off-road trails & quiet Lanes

cycling in the Lake District & yorkshire Dales

written by **keith Bradbury**

VERTEBRATE **GRAPHICS**
PUBLISHING

Design and production by Vertebrate Graphics Ltd, Sheffield
www.v-graphics.co.uk/publications

off-road trails & quiet Lanes

cycling in the Lake district & yorkshire dales   written by keith bradbury

Cover photo by Andy Heading:
All photography by Andy Heading unless stated

VERTEBRATE **GRAPHICS**
PUBLISHING

Design & production by Paul Mellor
Edited by Tom Fenton
Vertebrate Graphics Ltd.
www.**v-graphics**.co.uk/publications

contents

INTRODUCTION

This guidebook is aimed at the cycling enthusiast, family riders and mountain bikers. People like me. People who enjoy cycling and don't mind putting in a bit of effort in pursuit of enjoyable downhill runs and good views, but who expect to be able to walk without assistance at the end of the trip! It is a book of easy(ish) bike rides.

I wrote this book out of personal need. Let me be frank. I am no longer a fit young man. My body has seen better days and my intake of food and wine does not help when transporting a fixed mass (me) from A to B.

I needed a book to suggest some genuinely enjoyable cycle rides. Rides on quiet lanes and bridleways that I could ride with my friends or with my 15-year-old daughter. Routes that would never be too hard or take too long but that would leave me with a grin on my face and a spring in my step.

If you are the sort of rider who refuses to get off and push when the going gets tough, can hop on one wheel or likes his or her heart rate beating at 3000 BPM for hours on end then this book will probably not push you to the levels you seek.

If, however, you want to escape for a couple of hours on a Sunday afternoon to get wet, muddy and mildly knackered or if your kids have brought their bikes with them on holiday and are pestering you to take them for a ride, this book is just what you need. It is unashamedly a book of cycle routes for the 'energetically challenged'.

Have fun! I hope to meet you out there sometime! I'll be the one pushing up the hill...

Keith Bradbury

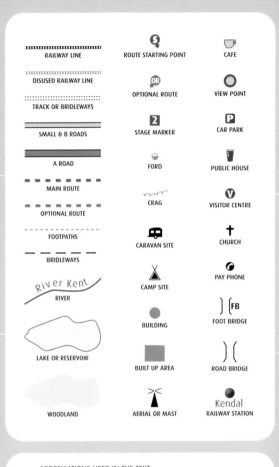

RAILWAY LINE	⚲ **ROUTE STARTING POINT**	☕ **CAFE**
DISUSED RAILWAY LINE	**OR** **OPTIONAL ROUTE**	◎ **VIEW POINT**
TRACK OR BRIDLEWAYS	**2** **STAGE MARKER**	**P** **CAR PARK**
SMALL & B ROADS	🛟 **FORD**	🍺 **PUBLIC HOUSE**
A ROAD	**CRAG**	**V** **VISITOR CENTRE**
MAIN ROUTE	🚐 **CARAVAN SITE**	✝ **CHURCH**
OPTIONAL ROUTE	⛺ **CAMP SITE**	☎ **PAY PHONE**
FOOTPATHS	● **BUILDING**	) (FB **FOOT BRIDGE**
BRIDLEWAYS	■ **BUILT UP AREA**	) (**ROAD BRIDGE**
River Kent **RIVER**		
LAKE OR RESERVOIR	📡 **AERIAL OR MAST**	● Kendal **RAILWAY STATION**
WOODLAND		

ABBREVIATIONS USED IN THE TEXT

L | **LH** | **R** | **RH** | **SA**
LEFT TURN | LEFT-HAND | RIGHT TURN | RIGHT-HAND | STRAIGHT AHEAD

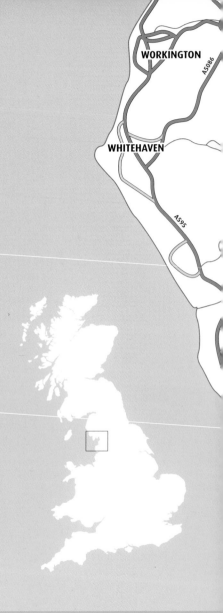

WORKINGTON

A5086

WHITEHAVEN

A595

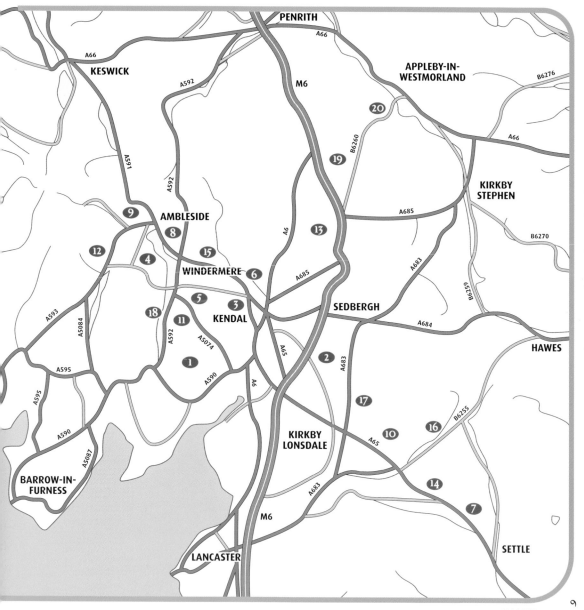

a note on the rides

This book is aimed at the beginner or intermediate cyclist. Although all of the routes can be completed by the novice cyclist, you can expect to have to put in a bit of effort occasionally. Some of the climbs are steep and the off-road descents can be rough and ready. That's just down to the nature of the terrain in the Yorkshire Dales and the Lake District. Treat it as a challenge and you'll have a great time.

I have tried to grade the routes in order of difficulty – easier at the start of the book and getting harder towards the rear. Even the hardest routes have been completed by my 15-year-old daughter, on a modestly priced bike bought from a well-known high street store, so don't worry too much!

Most rides are circular, starting and finishing at an appropriate place with convenient parking. I have aimed to keep the harder climbs on tarmac and to move off-road for the descents. (Of course, you could choose to ride all the routes in reverse!) A couple of the routes are linear. This causes some inconvenience in that you need to make plans to get back to your starting point, but the routes have been included as they are well worth the extra arrangements involved.

Each route is a mixture of quiet, virtually traffic-free lanes and bridleways of varying degrees of steepness and rideability. The first couple of routes can be completed entirely on tarmac with only optional off-road content. If you are new to cycling, my suggestion is that you try the tarmac route first to see how your bum copes with the stress and then come back on another occasion to tackle the off-road variation. Once you have a couple of routes under your belt, you can feel reassured that the next few routes in the book should be well within your capabilities.

your bike

Any bike will get you round the road rides in this book, provided it works. It you're going to venture off-road, I'd recommend a mountain bike, as the increased toughness and comfort will pay dividends. Check everything works - you won't be going anywhere fast if your gears seize, but you'll probably be a little quicker than planned if your brakes fail... Pump the tyres up, check they aren't about to wear through and ensure that everything that should be tight is tight. If you're not sure you can do this yourself, visit your local bike shop.

clothing

You need to get your clothing right if you want to stay comfortable on a bike, especially in bad weather.

Ideally, you want to be wearing clothing made from 'technical' synthetic or wool fabrics, which 'wick' or draw the sweat away from your body and then dry quickly, preventing you from getting cold and damp. (Stay away from cotton, as it absorbs moisture and then holds onto it.) If it's chilly, wear a layer of thin fleece on top to keep you warm, and then a wind/waterproof on top of this, to keep out the elements.

As cycling is an active sport, it's worth setting off just a little on the cool side - you'll soon warm up. Don't leave the warm clothes behind though, as the weather could turn and they'll keep you warm on lunch stops.

helmet

"The best helmet is the one that you're wearing", but please, make sure it fits, you're wearing it correctly and that it won't move around in a crash...

gloves

Cycling gloves help prevent blisters and numb hands and keep your fingers warm. They also provide a surprising amount of protection if you come off.

other essentials

As mentioned, take any necessary spares, tools and a pump. We'd also recommend taking a spare inner tube, as it's far quicker to swop tubes than to stop and repair a puncture. (Just be aware that if your kids are along for the ride, their bikes may have smaller wheels than yours and thus need different tubes!) Also consider spare clothes, a first aid kit and make sure you have enough food and water. Stop short of the kitchen sink, as you'll still want to be able to actually ride your bike.

You'll need something to carry this little lot in. We'd suggest a rucksack as they keep excess weight off the bike. Many suitable rucksacks are now compatible with water 'bladders' which allow you to drink on the move via a tube and mouthpiece. Whatever you choose, make sure it's big enough to carry everything, including any excess clothing you may be wearing.

maps

These rides are covered by:

Ordnance Survey: OL 7 – The English Lakes, South-eastern area, OL 2 – The Yorkshire Dales, Southern and Western areas, OL 41 – Forest of Bowland and Ribblesdale, OL 19 – Howgill Fells & Upper Eden Valley

Harvey Maps: Yorkshire Dales East, Yorkshire Dales South, Lakeland Central, Lakeland East, Lakeland South East

BMC: Waterproof Lake District map – www.v-graphics.co.uk/publications

Note: Maps, Descriptions, Distances
While every effort has been made to maintain accuracy within the maps and descriptions in this guide, we have had to process a vast amount of information and we are unable to guarantee that every single detail is correct.

Please exercise caution if a direction appears at odds with the route on the map. If in doubt, a comparison between the route, the description and a quick cross-reference to your map (along with a bit of common sense) should help ensure that you're on the right track. Note that distances have been measured from the map – these may not tally with your bike computer as map distances rarely coincide 100% with distances on the ground (and you may have to carry your bike at times). Please treat stated distances as a guideline only.

general safety (a.k.a. 'common sense')

Cycling can be dangerous. Too much exuberance on a descent in the middle of nowhere could leave you in more than a spot of bother. Consider your limitations and relative fragility before launching at something.

Carry food and water, spares, a tube and pump. Consider a first-aid kit. Even if it's warm, the weather could turn, so take a wind/waterproof. Think about what could happen on an enforced stop. Pack lights if you could finish in the dark, (as over-ambitious family trips often do!).

The ability to map-read, navigate and understand weather warnings is essential. Don't go out in bad weather unless you're confident and capable of doing so.

While these routes keep to quiet lanes as much as is possible, roads in this region can be very busy. Plan accordingly, obey the Highway Code and assume the majority of drivers are idiots...

If riding alone, think about the potential seriousness of an accident – you could be without help for a long time. Tell someone where you're going and when you'll be back. Take a phone if you have one, but don't rely on getting a signal. (And don't call out mountain rescue because you've grazed your knee.)

Riding in a group is safer (ambitious overtaking manoeuvres excepted) and often more fun, but don't leave slower riders behind and give them a breather when they've caught up.

As the area is popular, ride in control and give way to others. Bells might be annoying, but they work. If you can't bring yourself to bolt one on, a polite 'excuse me' should be fine.

On hot, sunny days, make sure that you slap some Factor 30+ and **ALWAYS WEAR YOUR HELMET!**

Mountain Rescue
In the event of an accident requiring mountain rescue assistance:
Dial 999 and ask for POLICE – MOUNTAIN RESCUE.

A basic knowledge of first aid, a map to provide mountain rescue with your location and warm clothing will all be of great help in an emergency.

off-road rights of way

essentially, you are allowed on:

Bridleways (blue arrows on signposts)
Mountain bikers have the right to share bridleways with walkers and horses – but take care, horses spook easily.

Byways Open to All Traffic (Red arrows)
Otherwise known as BOATs, these allow all traffic to pass, including vehicles – although, surprisingly, I've yet to see a boat on a BOAT. This means that you may well be sharing the trail with motorcyclists and 4WD enthusiasts – often to be seen enjoying the peace, quiet and fresh air of the countryside.

Forest Tracks and Paths
Officially, you need permission to ride through Forestry Commission land. Often, however, this permission has already been granted, and the Forestry Commission generally regards cycling favourably. A note of caution – beware of forestry operations, because a fully loaded logging truck could easily dent your bike!

Green Lanes
A non-legal term for an unsurfaced country road. There is some debate as to who's allowed to use them, but mountain bikers have nothing to worry about at present.

White Roads
Most roads on maps have colours that indicate their status, white roads have no colour and so have no recorded right of way status. These often appear to be farm tracks or private roads when, in fact, they are public highways. Of the estimated 7000km of 'lost' white roads around the UK, many give great, totally legal cycling. Unfortunately, you need to check with the definitive map at your local highway authority to be absolutely sure. If in doubt stick to a bridleway.

NB. This doesn't mean that you take precedence over other trail users, just that you're allowed to be there. You should still give way to walkers, and horseriders. If you're not already familiar with the symbols on your map denoting bridleways, footpaths and so on, check the information section on your map.

and you're not allowed on:

Footpaths (Yellow arrows)
They might look tempting, but steer clear. They're likely to be full of stiles and slow-moving walkers at any rate.

Everywhere else!
Literally – walkers may well be allowed to roam wherever they please, but cyclists cannot.

Signs

Not all footpaths and bridleways are signed. This means that there is not necessarily any clear indication 'on the ground' as to whether that wide trail that you want to follow is an illegal footpath or a legal bridleway. That's why it's a good idea to carry a map with you on every ride.

Rules of the (off) road

- Always ride on legal trails.
- Ride considerately – give way to horses and pedestrians.
- Don't spook animals.
- Ride in control – you don't know who's around the next corner.
- Leave gates as you find them – if you're unsure, shut them.
- Keep the noise down and don't swear loudly when you fall off in front of walkers.
- Leave no trace – take home everything you took out.
- Keep water sources clean – don't take toilet stops near streams.
- Enjoy the countryside and respect its life and work.

the winster valley

route 1 // 16.9km (10.5 miles)

The Winster valley lies between the tourist honey pots of Kendal and Newby Bridge. Leave the crowds behind and let the tourist traffic fly on by – this little gem is largely left to those who care to search more carefully.

A flat route (by Lake District standards), this ride takes you on a clockwise loop of the lanes running along the base of the valley, with an optional off-road section adding some pleasant woodland trails and a fabulous descent. The other distinct bonus of this route is that it starts and finishes at... that's right, a pub! In fact, you have a choice of two: The Hare and Hounds at Bowland Bridge or The Masons Arms, a little further up the hill at Strawberry Bank.

Assuming that you do not wish to cycle up Strawberry Bank at the end of your ride, we will start the description from The Hare and Hounds, which has a large car park alongside the pub (**please get permission from the landlord** before abandoning your car and disappearing in a cloud of dust). For those of you not planning to visit the pub, there is ample parking to be found in the area.

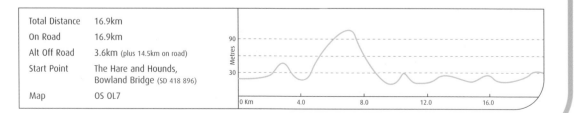

Total Distance	16.9km
On Road	16.9km
Alt Off Road	3.6km (plus 14.5km on road)
Start Point	The Hare and Hounds, Bowland Bridge (SD 418 896)
Map	OS OL7

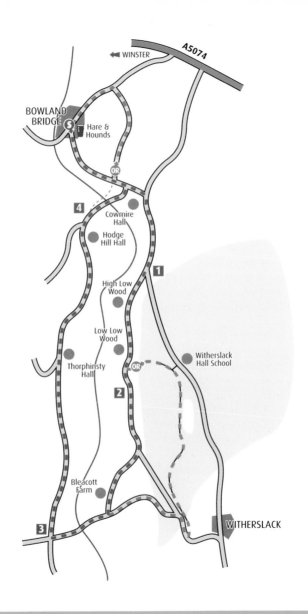

From the car park, cycle past the front of the pub then turn immediately **L** along a quiet lane. Ignore all side junctions until the road passes through a farm and you come to a halt at a T-junction. Turn **R** at the junction and continue gently uphill until the hamlet of Pool Bank is reached. Climb up past the last house to the crest of the hill where the road splits. This is the high point of the route and the beginning of a welcome downhill section.

1 Bear **R** at the junction to run steeply downhill, then through open countryside, past farms at High Low Wood, Middle Low Wood and yes, you guessed it, Low Low Wood! (They were stunningly imaginative with place names in days gone by!) Just past the last farm, (Low Low Wood) the road turns **L** and starts to rise again. A little further on, the road turns sharp **R** again at Knot Wood, and at this point, a bridleway goes off **L** into the wood. This is the off-road option and is described at the end of this route description.

2 Meanwhile, continue on the road, gently uphill, (you always have to pay for these exhilarating downhills you know), through more picturesque scenery and farmsteads, bearing **R** at the junction, until the road runs downhill again and levels out on the valley floor. Pleasant riding continues, past Bleacott Farm, until a T-junction is met. (The road coming in from your **L** here is the end of the off-road variation. From this point, both routes share the same description.) Turn **R**, cross the River Winster and climb a short but steep hill (Holme Road) to the brow. This is a good place to stop to rest your aching limbs and gasping lungs whilst pretending to everyone else that you are just admiring the views along the valley.

A fine downhill section follows to a crossroads. Left goes along the valley to Lindale village, whilst the way back to the start is to the right. Straight ahead at the crossroads is up a VERY steep hill and therefore should be completely ignored!

3 Turning **R**, the route now follows the valley floor on the opposite side to that along which you have just laboriously pedalled. Glorious views with buzzards soaring overhead give ample compensation for the occasional short hill on the return journey.

Keep **SA** on the road, ignoring minor roads coming in from the left and sail gracefully past farms at Low Tarn Green, High Tarn Green and Thorphinsty Hall. After 5.4km, you reach Hodge Hill Farm, where you need to bear **R** at the junction. A further 1.3km brings you to the end of the road at a T-junction as Cowmire Hall comes once more into view. This is the road you cycled out on at the beginning of the ride.

4 Turn **L** at the junction, over a small rise and then it is time to make a decision. Continue along this road and Bowland Bridge is reached in 1km or so by re-tracing your original route. Alternatively, (and only slightly longer), once over the small rise, take the first road on the **R** and follow it along further pleasant terrain (Woodside Road) until it reaches a busier road at a T-junction. Turn **L** at the junction, over a final small rise to drop down to Bowland Bridge after 1km.

Optional route: From the bridleway junction identified earlier at Knot Wood, follow a rising track through the woods towards Witherslack Hall School. The track is steep and rocky at first but can be ridden in its entirety if you are so inclined. (Sorry about the pun... going uphill? So inclined? Oh, suit yourselves!)

The gradient soon eases off to give easy, pleasant riding through mixed woodland, rising steadily to a sudden clearing where a residential school, Witherslack Hall comes into view, hidden away in its own secret valley. Ignore the roads going down to the Hall or the associated farm buildings, and turn **R** instead, (just before hitting the road), along a good access track which leads out into open fields near a few cottages.

Don't take the track going left towards the cottages but follow the other good track which bears **R** to a gate in the corner of the field ahead. This track enters more mixed woodland giving easy riding until you break out into more open terrain with a number of paths going off ahead. The tendency is to take the lower path going more or less straight ahead (because the other one goes uphill). In fact, the track going uphill, to the **R**, is the correct path, as it climbs gently past Yewbarrow crag and onto a gate and signpost, allowing access through the drystone wall ahead. Don't worry if you keep too low in this field, you will quickly come across the opposite boundary wall, and a **R** turn will take you up to the correct route on one of the numerous paths that criss-cross this area.

Once through the gate, an excellent track begins a fabulous descent down through the wood. A hard-packed mud surface with the odd tree root and rocky section adding extra interest makes up for all the hard work in getting up here. The route descends steadily and eventually drops out (literally) onto the tarmac road in Witherslack village – a fine descent!

Turn **R** along the road but quickly take the first **L**, past the entrance to Halecat Garden Centre, and continue on past Fern Hill on the Bleacrag Road.

Just before the bridge over the River Winster, a minor road joins from your right. This is the road where those doing the tarmac route will join up and both routes now share the same description as they continue over the bridge and up the short, steep hill ahead.

OLD HUTTON
& KILLINGTON Lake

ROUTE 2 // 18.9km (11.7 miles)

Killington Lake (or more correctly Killington Reservoir) **was originally built to feed water into the Lancaster to Kendal Canal. The lake is now a peaceful haven tucked into a beautiful pastoral landscape in area that gives the opportunity for many excellent routes on quiet and picturesque lanes.**

This route explores the lanes and back roads between the lake and the village of Old Hutton. The main route is entirely on tarmac but an excellent off-road variation is also described. Buzzards, deer, badger and a profusion of wildfowl are all to be found in the area. Take your binoculars and enjoy a wonderful afternoon ride in peaceful meditation.

One can, of course, start the ride in Kendal and cycle out to the starting point. Unfortunately, Kendal is in the valley – and the area we are interested in is considerably higher! Much more convenient is to drive up to Old Hutton and begin the ride from there.

Take the B6254 (commonly known as the back road to Kirkby Lonsdale) out of Kendal, past Oxenholme railway station and continue to the village of Old Hutton. Continue through the village until a hill leads up to a crossroads, where you turn **L**. If you reach a bridge carrying the M6 motorway over the B road, you have gone approximately 100m too far. The road climbs a small hill then crosses over the M6. Park anywhere in this area.

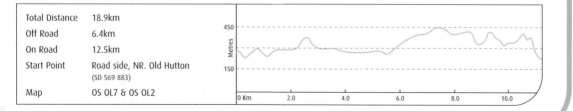

Total Distance	18.9km
Off Road	6.4km
On Road	12.5km
Start Point	Road side, NR. Old Hutton (SD 569 883)
Map	OS OL7 & OS OL2

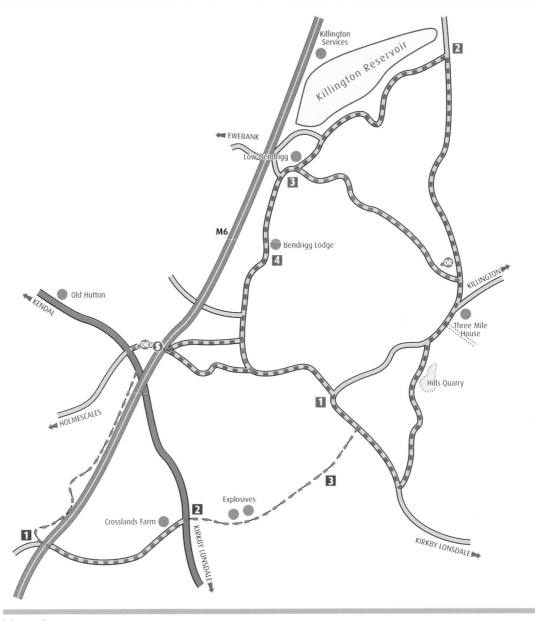

Killington Services

Killington Reservoir

2

EWEBANK

Low Bendrigg

3

M6

Bendrigg Lodge

4

Old Hutton

KENDAL

OR S

HOLMESCALES

KILLINGTON

OR

Three Mile House

Hills Quarry

1

KIRKBY LONSDALE

1

2

Crosslands Farm

Explosives

3

KIRKBY LONSDALE

The route begins by crossing the M6 on the flyover you have just parked next to. Continue along this pleasant, undulating road past small copses (copses – not corpses) until a small, pump station is passed on the right and the road splits at a large tree called the Hanging Tree! I'm sure that some local historian will be able to tell you why it is called the Hanging Tree but, then again, its much more likely that someone has been telling me a load of rubbish and I fell for it hook, line and sinker.

1 Anyway, at the Hanging Tree, take the **R** fork along a further pleasant lane, watching out for a bridleway sign on the **R** of the road. If you come back to attempt the optional, off-road section of this route, this is where you will pop out onto tarmac.

From here, the road drops a little then climbs a further slight rise to where a narrow road goes off **L**. This is our route onwards. More pleasant, undulating terrain follows, passing a small nature reserve on the left and a disused quarry on the right.

Ignoring the road coming in on the left, (this goes back up to the Hanging Tree junction!) continue gently uphill past a farm (Three Mile House), to a staggered junction. Our route goes **SA** at the first part of the junction whilst the right branch goes steeply upwards to Killington village.

Optional route: If you're already feeling tired, turning **L** at the second junction knocks a couple of km off the distance.

Continuing **SA**, climb a couple of short but steep hills, and drop down a pleasant downhill section on the other side. Resist the temptation to break the world land speed record at this point because you will need to watch out for a **L** turn at the base of the hill.

2 Taking the **L** turn, the road is now very quiet indeed and runs tranquilly alongside Killington Lake. Pass the boats and houses at the end then drop down a small hill, keeping **R** at the bottom, to run parallel to the main dam wall. The road now swings back **L** and up a short climb.

3 The road drops down through a farm, passes a junction on the left, (this is where the earlier, shortened route rejoins) and begins to climb up a short hill to Bendrigg Lodge. As you start the climb at the base of this hill, ignore the road going off to the right and bear **L** on the main road.

Bendrigg Lodge is an outdoor activity centre for disadvantaged youngsters and would always be glad of a donation as you pass by, if you are feeling particularly flush!

4 Past Bendrigg, drop down the hill (watch the sharp bend at the bottom) then continue over a small bridge to a junction. Turning **R** at the junction climbs a steep, lung-busting, calf-stretching hill leading directly to the motorway bridge and your car. Alternatively, **SA**, and **R** at the next T-junction brings you out at the same place by means of a longer, but more gentle climb.

Optional route: Don't cross the motorway at the start of the route but instead drop back down the hill to the crossroads and turn **L**. Now climb the hill up to the motorway bridge but **do not go under it**. On the **R** (immediately alongside the motorway embankment) is a bridleway which follows the motorway and provides an entertaining variation to our route. The first section of the track is used by the farm for access and is likely to be liberally strewn with what is colloquially known as 'cowsh'. (No, I don't know what it means either!) The lane is easily rideable on a good surface and climbs steadily before dropping gently downwards, giving an enjoyable run in a bizarre situation with open fields on one side and the hard shoulder of the M6 about 6m to your left!

Follow the track as it veers away from the motorway then swings back **L** to run alongside it again. If in doubt, take the track that keeps you nearer the Motorway until, after a sharp **LH** bend in fields, a slight rise brings you to a gate, opening out onto a quiet tarmac road.

1 Turn **L** to pass under the motorway and leave it behind as you climb a long, steady hill – payback for the pleasant downhill run you have just enjoyed!

At last the road levels out and a couple of isolated houses are passed at Crosslands Farm. At this point, a T-junction is reached and you need to take the bridleway **SA** – through the gate directly opposite.

2 The first section of the bridleway is easy riding on tarmac and gravel past some peculiar buildings which I am led to believe are explosives stores for a local quarry – but hey, what do I know? I believed that they used to hang people on the Hanging Tree!

Route finding is very straightforward until, a little way beyond the last of the ammunition stores, a gate is reached and the track can be seen heading across the field ahead. Follow the track but watch carefully here for the prominent remains of an old ruined wall. As the track crosses the wall, leave the track and follow the line of the wall, across small streams and around the base of a prominent bluff. The track becomes easier to follow as an old gate (in urgent need of repair) is reached.

3 The bridleway now gives pleasant riding over mixed terrain, getting a little boggy and indistinct towards the latter stages until, at a gate, you will pop out onto a quiet road, a few hundred metres past the – yes, you guessed it – the Hanging Tree! You have now rejoined the main route at **2**

Lakes & Dales

keNDaL
to sizergh castLe
ROUTE 3 // 14.5km (9 mILes)

A few miles to the South West of Kendal lies the National Trust property of Sizergh Castle. The castle and gardens are open to the public, and well worth a visit (check opening times before setting off – tel. 01539 560 951 – although you can ride this route irrespective of whether the grounds are open or closed). More to the point, there are some excellent bridleways which climb steadily to a fantastic viewpoint at Helsington Church, looking down across the flood plains to the estuary at Arnside and the mountains of the Lake District a little further off in the distance. More exhilarating riding then leads down to the castle itself before the return to Kendal enjoys a leisurely amble back alongside the river on pleasant tracks in the delightful Kent valley.

Begin the ride from the Kendal Leisure Centre on Burton Road. (Follow signs for the A65 Kirkby Lonsdale.) Plenty of free parking is available alongside the River Kent at the start of the road to Sedgwick and Natland, just off the roundabout near the Leisure Centre.

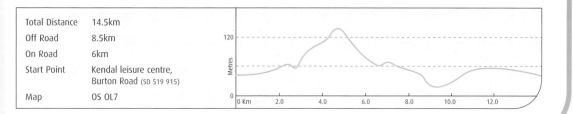

Total Distance	14.5km
Off Road	8.5km
On Road	6km
Start Point	Kendal leisure centre, Burton Road (SD 519 915)
Map	OS OL7

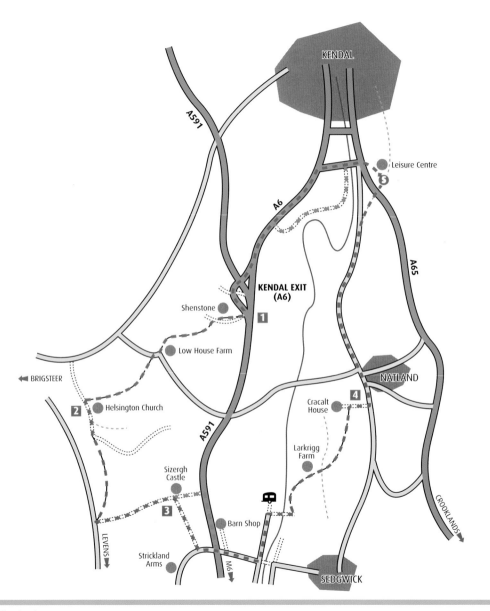

KENDAL

A591

A6

KENDAL EXIT
(A6)

1

Leisure Centre

5

A65

Shenstone

Low House Farm

◄◄ BRIGSTEER

2 Helsington Church

A591

NATLAND

4

Cracalt House

Larkrigg Farm

Sizergh Castle

3

Barn Shop

LEVENS

Strickland Arms

M6

CROOKLANDS

SEDGWICK

With your back to the leisure centre, turn **R** and go down to the roundabout next to the bridge across the river (Romney Bridge). Take the second exit and cross the river, following Romney Road up to the traffic lights at the junction of Romney Road and Milnthorpe Road. Turn **L** at the lights and follow the A6 out of Kendal, past the Kendal Arms and Stonecross Manor Hotel.

Optional (quieter) route out of Kendal:
Immediately over the bridge, turn **L** alongside the river and follow a quiet road into a residential area. Turn **L** at the first junction then **L** again onto Bellingham Road and follow it as it weaves through the estate. Look out for the **R** turn into Kent Park Avenue, which climbs a small hill to meet the main road just before (the now disused) Helsington filling station. Turn **L**, rejoining the main route.

Once past the filling station site at Helsington, the footpath/cycle path alongside the busy main road becomes wide enough to cycle along. Continue as far as the large roundabout where the Kendal road joins the Kendal bypass (the dual carriageway).

1 The roundabout is complex and can be busy, so take great care when crossing. Take the exit which goes underneath the main bypass (signposted Windermere and Shenstone) and follow the slip road as it circles around to the left. Just before the slip road reaches the main carriageway, a small access road goes off to the **R**, signposted Shenstone.

Take this lane, which very quickly crosses the busy exit slip road, taking traffic off the bypass and into Kendal. This is now the end of the traffic-filled roads. From here, the route is either off-road or makes use of very quiet and peaceful roads and tracks.

Once over the slip road, the access lane climbs a small hill to the entrance to Shenstone House. Keep **L** here and find a narrow bridleway that runs uphill between hedges to a gate. Through the gate, the path breaks out into open fields and the track can be clearly seen, crossing the field diagonally **L** to a gate in the top corner.

From here, a rutted lane is followed steeply uphill, to reach a concrete farm track which zig zags down and through a farmyard to reach a narrow country lane.

Turn **R**, climbing gently uphill, and take a bridleway on the **L** at the end of the farm buildings, signposted Helsington Church. This track passes a cottage on the left before going through a farm gate into open fields. Follow the track as it first climbs to a gate by a tree, then drops down to another gate in the **LH** corner of a muddy field. The stony track then follows a wall on the left to meet the access road to Helsington Church at a fantastic viewpoint, looking down over Lord's Plain, Whitbarrow Scar and Morecambe Bay. Relax peacefully here, safe in the knowledge that virtually all the climbing is over and the downhill sections are still to come.

2 After enjoying the views, continue **SA** along the track, passing the church on the left and ignoring any alternative tracks until you reach a sharp **LH** bend in the track. Immediately ahead is a gate into a field. Go **SA** through this gate and follow the bridleway sign into the field. At the far end of the field, the track drops down a stony section and through a gate with an unusual catch. Follow the distinctive track to the **R** then back **L** into a very large field with a fenced copse of trees in the centre.

The track is lost in this field but, from the top of the hill, head downhill and diagonally to the right of the copse to meet a very prominent farm track running along the entire lower edge of the field. Turn **L** along this track. (Do not go through the gate in the corner of the field onto the road!) Follow the field wall along the bottom of the hill until it swings around to the **R** and encounters two further gates.

N.B. The farm track you have just ridden along and subsequent section through the Sizergh Estate is not officially classified as a bridleway and is accessed through the kind permission of the Sizergh Castle Estate Office, who will not object if you cycle sensibly along it. This is strictly on the understanding that they accept no responsibility for any mishaps which may occur as the track is not maintained and cyclists go along it at their own risk. Furthermore it is not a formal right of way and the Estate Office may withdraw this permission at any time. Please remember that, as always, animals and pedestrians have right of way at all times.

3 The continuation of this lane to Sizergh Castle is through the **RH** of the two gates you have just met, but this short section is designated a footpath and **MUST NOT** be cycled at the moment. Discussions on the re-designation of this footpath are in progress and it may be that, in the near future, cycling will be permissible along this section. Until then, obey the no cycling signs and push up the very short rise and down to the car park.

You will, no doubt, wish to avail yourself of the hospitality offered within the castle estate. When you are ready to move on again, ease your aching limbs out of that comfy chair and push your trusty steed through the visitor areas, until the access road on the other side of the cattle grid has been reached. Follow the exit signs through the estate grounds, bearing **R** where the road forks at the bottom of the short hill. Negotiate the speed bumps and cattle grid to arrive at the main gates of the estate.

N.B. In the **extremely** unlikely event of these gates being locked during out-of season hours, return to the junction a little further back and take the **LH** fork which exits onto the A591. Walk very carefully back down the grass verge for a little way to the large roundabout at Brettargh Holt and follow signs to Sizergh Castle and the Strickland Arms. This will bring you to the OTHER side of the problematic gates, but the gates are only locked when wholly unforeseen situations demand it. (Foot & Mouth outbreaks etc.)

Immediately through the gates, turn **L** to pass under the Kendal bypass (A591) and pass the entry to Sizergh Barn, farm shop and tearooms on the left. Continue steeply down the quiet road (Nannypie Lane) to meet the River Kent at a T-junction.

The brave and the foolhardy can attempt to cross the river by the ford, which goes straight ahead at the T-junction. You are extremely unlikely to get across the river without getting VERY wet and **don't even think about** attempting it in high water conditions.

Otherwise, turn **L** at the T-junction, signposted to a caravan park. Just before the entrance to the caravan site, a signpost on the right points to the entrance of an attractive suspension footbridge over the river. (Push your bikes across the footbridge.)

A **L** turn after the footbridge follows the river past attractive picnic spots to a gate leading onto a dirt track. The bridleway soon swings **R**, following the track away from the river, (a footpath goes to the left).

A sharp **R** turn leads to a gate into an open field at Larkrigg Farm. Head diagonally **R** across the field, aiming for the old canal bridge on top of the embankment. (The canal towpath can be followed back to Kendal but this is a footpath only and should not be cycled.) The bridleway climbs up the short, steep bank onto the bridge and crosses the canal, following the original gravel farm track. This track quickly reaches the modern farm access road, which is followed uphill (away from the farm) to where the road turns sharp **R** on a little rise. Leave the track at this point and continue **SA**, downhill, on a singletrack bridleway, to reach a gate at the bottom of a short hill. Continue through the gate, up a short rise and onto a tarmac road at the entrance to Cracalt Farm.

4 Turn **R** up the lane to quickly reach the Sedgwick/ Natland road. Turn **L** onto this road, past Holme's Garden Centre and follow the main road through the village and onto the outskirts of Kendal in less than 2.5km.

A prominent line of large Poplar and Leylandii trees, forming a screen for the K Shoes factory buildings, marks the outskirts of Kendal. Look carefully on the **R** to find the canal path cycle way, which can be followed, crossing the busy Burton Road and then continuing to reach the Leisure Centre car park after a few more yards.

BOWNESS
to AMBLESIDE

ROUTE 4 // 14.7km (9.1 MILES)

A glance at the map will show a number of bridleways running alongside the western shore of Windermere, between the ferry at Bowness and the top of the lake at Ambleside. However, the map does not tell the whole story. It is possible to cycle, on well-surfaced tracks in a lovely setting, alongside the lake from the ferry landing at Ferry House all the way up to Wray Castle and then on roads into Ambleside, before jumping onto one of the Windermere steamers that ply their trade up and down the lake and having a nice cup of tea as you sail serenely back down the lake to your car. Yes, I know it's cheating, but for a pleasant, easy afternoon's outing, involving very moderate climbing in a fantastic setting, it doesn't really get much better than this!

Start the ride from any of the many car parks in and around Bowness then cycle down to the Steamer jetty area known as the Glebe.

The ferry we need to catch across the lake is the Windermere Car Ferry, which docks one kilometre to the south of the pedestrian ferries in Bowness.

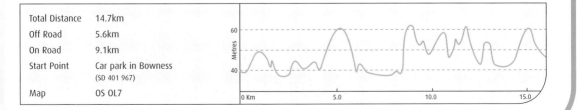

Total Distance	14.7km
Off Road	5.6km
On Road	9.1km
Start Point	Car park in Bowness (SD 401 967)
Map	OS OL7

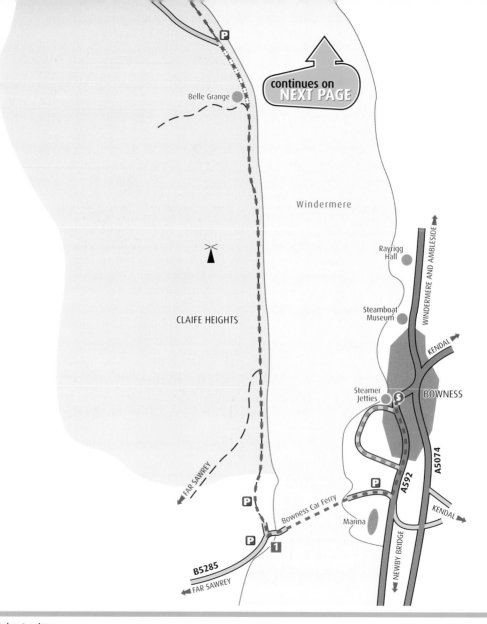

continues on NEXT PAGE

Windermere

Belle Grange

Rayrigg Hall

Steamboat Museum

CLAIFE HEIGHTS

WINDERMERE AND AMBLESIDE

KENDAL

Steamer Jetties

S

BOWNESS

A592

A5074

KENDAL

FAR SAWREY

Bowness Car Ferry

Marina

NEWBY BRIDGE

B5285

FAR SAWREY

1

From the steamer jetties, the main road (A592) can be followed directly out of Bowness towards Newby Bridge and the Windermere Car Ferry. Alternatively, a small road leads off to the **R** along the edge of the lake, past numerous shops, ice cream parlours and boat houses to turn **R** when it rejoins the A592 a little further along towards the ferry. Turn **R** onto the B5285, just before the marina and following the signs to the car ferry, to join the inevitable queue of cars. Fortunately, a bike does not count as a car, so cycle serenely past the waiting hordes to the head of the queue and enjoy your trip across the lake to the other side.

1 From the opposite landing stage, the road winds first **L** then back **R** around a small headland. After a short distance, turn **R** at a sharp **LH** bend, onto a narrow, tarmac lane. Follow this as it runs through woodland then into more open terrain in a very attractive situation with the lake on your right.

Eventually the tarmac runs out and you continue **SA** onto a well-graded (if sometimes muddy) track that continues to run alongside the lake for about 3km. Ignore the occasional bridleway which climbs off to the left up onto Claife Heights (these are for another day).

Eventually, a smoother, gravel surface is reached through a gate at the drive to Belle Grange. Ignoring the bridleway on the left, (I've already told you about these!), ride **SA** along the gravel lane until you hit tarmac and begin to rise more steeply. At this point, look out for a small car park and bridleway on the **R** at Red Nab, which you need to take as it drops down into woods and runs alongside the lake, past a jetty at Balla Wray and onto a ford at High Wray Bay.

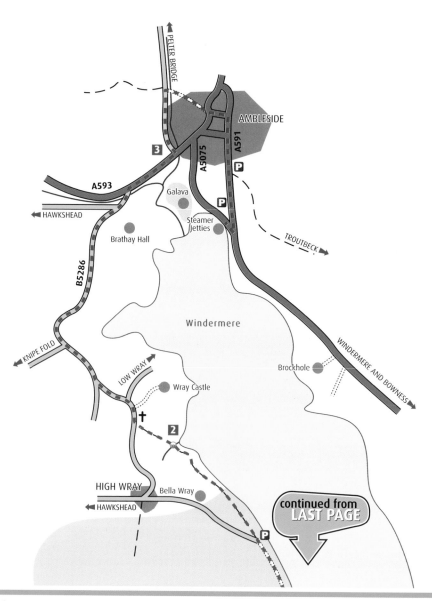

PELTER BRIDGE

AMBLESIDE

3

A593

A5075

A591

HAWKSHEAD

Galava

P

P

Steamer
Jetties

Brathay Hall

TROUTBECK

B5286

Windermere

KNIPE FOLD

Brockhole

WINDERMERE AND BOWNESS

LOW WRAY

Wray Castle

†

2

HIGH WRAY

Bella Wray

HAWKSHEAD

continued from
LAST PAGE

P

2 The track leaves the lake and begins to climb the hill to break out onto the road from High Wray to Low Wray. Turn **R** here, passing the church and the Lodge House of Wray Castle. A little further down the road, ignore the road off to the right to Low Wray. Your road soon meets the much busier B5286 at a T-junction. Turn **R** here and follow the B5286 to a bridge over the River Brathay at Clappersgate then turn **R** onto the A593 to another bridge across the River Rothay – a total distance of 3km from the church at Wray.

3 **Do not cross this second bridge**. Instead, turn **L** immediately before it onto a quiet back road and follow it alongside the River Rothay for just less than 1km. At this point, an obvious 'packhorse' footbridge crosses the river and leads into Rothay Park. A short walk (200m) through the park will bring you into the centre of Ambleside.

Having explored Ambleside, your return ferry leaves from the jetties at Waterhead (about 1km from the town centre) There are numerous ways to get to Waterhead but the easiest is to follow the A591, (signposted Windermere and Kendal) past a large Garden Centre and onto a junction controlled by traffic lights. This is Waterhead and the jetties are obvious on the right-hand side of the road along with the associated bustle of general tourist facilities.

If you don't wish to take the ferry back, you could continue along the A591 out of Ambleside, turning onto the A592 just before Windermere. However, this road is fast, very busy and **not** recommended.

ashes Lane
& Bell Hill

Just to the west of Kendal can be found the small (but beautifully formed) **Bell Hill. No rights of way cross the summit but its base is perfectly circumnavigated by a series of excellent bridleways. This cracking little route links these tracks to give fine riding in beautiful situations without the steep climbs usually associated with routes in the Lake District. This is an old favourite I return to time-after-time when I have a couple of hours to spare and fancy a quick burn on the bike!**

Start from a small parking space on the side of the road about 1km before Crook, immediately beyond the point where Capplerigg Lane goes off to the left.

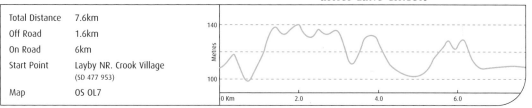

Total Distance	7.6km
Off Road	1.6km
On Road	6km
Start Point	Layby NR. Crook Village (SD 477 953)
Map	OS OL7

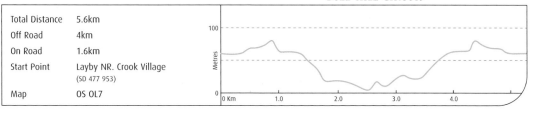

Total Distance	5.6km
Off Road	4km
On Road	1.6km
Start Point	Layby NR. Crook Village (SD 477 953)
Map	OS OL7

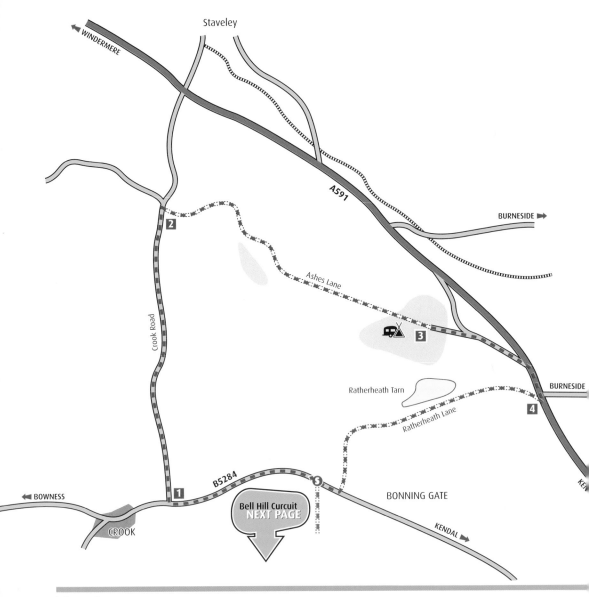

Staveley

WINDERMERE

A591

BURNESIDE ➡

2

Crook Road

Ashes Lane

3

BURNESIDE

Ratherheath Tarn

4

Ratherheath Lane

KEN

BOWNESS

1

B5284

5

Bell Hill Curcuit
NEXT PAGE

BONNING GATE

CROOK

KENDAL ➡

ashes Lane circuit

Head towards Crook along the relatively busy B5284. The road climbs a little then gives a fast downhill section, only to climb back up the other side to the outskirts of Crook village.

1 **DO NOT** drop down the hill into the village (unless you are heading for the Sun Inn for refreshments, of course). Our route turns **R** on the brow of the hill on the road to Staveley (shown as Crook Road on the map). The road climbs steadily at first but soon levels out and then drops gently downward again through very attractive countryside. After about 3km, the road begins to drop downwards more steeply into Staveley village, but our route goes off to the **R** before this happens – so save yourself the grief of having to slog back up the hill by being particularly vigilant at this point. A large, imposing house on the left of the road (New Hall) is a good landmark. The lane you are looking for (Ashes Lane) goes off to the **R** just past the point where the drive to New Hall meets the road.

2 Ashes Lane drops down a small hill to a cluster of houses (Ashes) then goes through a gate onto a pleasant track. A short uphill section meets another gate and open fields with the excellent track continuing ahead. Pleasant riding for about 1km reaches a further gate on the edge of Ashes Lane Caravan Park and the track continues to reach a quiet tarmac lane at the entrance to the site.

3 Continue along this lane until it rises slightly to reach a T-junction. Although the road you have just met looks like a normal road, it is actually a large layby, made from the remains of the original road to Windermere when the new bypass was built. Turn **R**, up the hill, to meet the aforementioned bypass after about 100m.

Please note: This short section of road is technically a one-way street. Traffic leaves the bypass to enter the layby and then must drive down the road to rejoin the bypass further down the hill. Because we are now heading uphill, against the flow of traffic, we should really be pushing our cycles so as not to break any traffic regulations.

On reaching the bypass, you have two choices:
A. cross the very busy, very fast and very dangerous dual carriageway, cycle 100m back towards Kendal on the correct side of the road and then re-cross the very busy, very fast and very dangerous dual carriageway to enter the very peaceful, very slow and very safe Ratherheath Lane; **or**
B. walk along the grass verge, against the flow of traffic, for 100m and turn **R** into Ratherheath Lane more simply and much more safely.

4 From this point, we leave all that intrusive traffic behind as we speed gently down the hill, past the highly photogenic Ratherheath Tarn and on to a T-junction. Turn **R** here onto the B5284 and climb over a small rise to meet your car at the end of the first loop of our figure-eight.

If you have now had enough, throw you bikes into your car, climb in yourself and speed off home! If, however, you are ready for more action, or if you have decided just to do the Bell Hill circuit, our next loop heads off down Capplerigg Lane, which should be just behind your car if you are parked in the correct spot! This lane is both the beginning and the end of our ride – it's so nice we decided to do it twice!

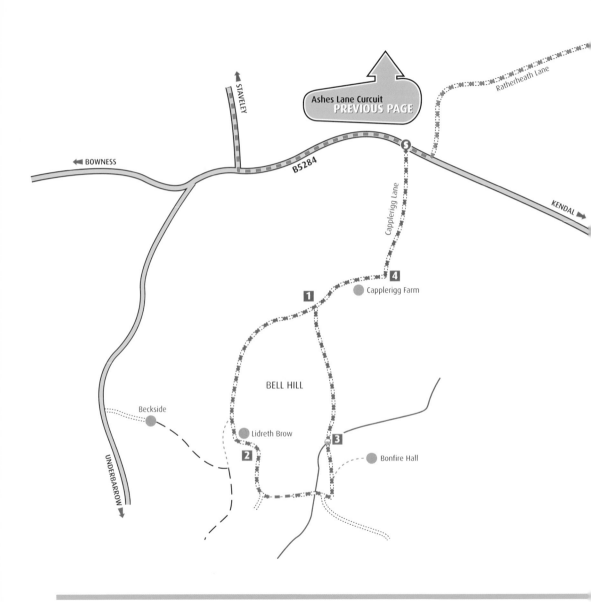

Ashes Lane Curcuit
PREVIOUS PAGE

Ratherheath Lane

◄◄ BOWNESS

STAVELEY

B5284

KENDAL ►►

Capplerigg Lane

5

4 ● Capplerigg Farm

1

BELL HILL

Beckside

2 ● Lidreth Brow

3

● Bonfire Hall

UNDERBARROW

BeLL HiLL CiRCUit

Capplerigg Lane climbs gently past a retirement home and up to a farm complex. Turn **R** on a clearly marked bridleway through a gate, just as the farm gates are reached. The bridleway drops down through another gate then climbs a small rise to a T-junction with a bridleway.

1 Our route turns **R** here, (signposted Lindreth Brow) to enjoy a fast descent on a very good, if rocky track. Down through mud and puddles, (this is what we came all this way for), until at the very bottom of the hill you meet a junction. **Ignore** the track which climbs to the right to a ruined barn (it's often difficult to spot anyway!). Instead, keep **L**, descend a little further, and follow the track round a **LH** bend to a large white cottage (Lindreth Brow).

2 Follow the easy track past a ruined building on the right covered in undergrowth, then to a gate into open fields. Our route turns almost immediately **L**, through another waymarked gate and up the grassy field ahead.

The bridleway goes **SA** up the hill, bearing gently to the **R** until, once on the top, the gate onwards is straight ahead of you as you drop down the other side. I used to walk round the edge of this field to prevent damage to the crops but, once got challenged (by the farmer?) for leaving the official path. Now straight up the field I go and have had no problem since! It's a funny old world isn't it?

From the gate, follow the wall on the left to a flat, muddy bridge over a stream. Through the gate and up the field ahead (following the hedge on the left) brings you to another gate and onto a farm lane.

Those of you who have ridden the Kendal to Windermere route will recognise the track leading uphill on your right to be the one you slithered down during that exciting adventure, but our route home today is the main farm track going **SA**.

Continue along the farm track, through a gate, and, **don't bear R** up to the farm. Keeping along the lower track brings you to another gate and a short section of lane to a ford.

3 This ford is eminently rideable, so if you fall off into the stream, it's your own silly fault. For the wimps, there is an attractive little slab bridge just to the right of the ford but its much more fun if you don't tell anyone about it until after they get wet!

Head uphill now, along the pleasant track. Some rocky areas may need the odd push but most of the lane can be ridden without difficulty. At the very top, another bridleway comes in from the right. You will, of course, recognise this track as being Capplerigg Lane which heads back through the farm and thence to your car, home and a well-deserved cuppa!

Longsleddale

route 6 // 16.8km (10.4 miles)

Eleven kilometres out of Kendal, along the A6 towards Shap, the valley of Longsleddale runs away to the left. It is a beautiful valley, luckily largely unknown to the throngs of tourists and has the added advantages of boasting a quiet and picturesque road running up the valley bottom and an excellent off-road bridleway coming back down. It is reputed to be the legendary Greendale – stomping ground of Postman Pat and his famous moggy, Jess. Pat's adventures are said to be set in and around this lovely valley, so watch out for a big red van driven by a guy with a huge nose and a massive black and white cat sat next to him! This route takes advantage of the quiet road, climbing gently for eight kilometres up to the hamlet of Sadgill, and then drops back down the valley on the bridleway to Garnett Bridge.

Parking in Garnett Bridge is limited, but turning **L** over the bridge onto the road to Burneside will find a number of spaces on the roadside, just on the outskirts of the hamlet.

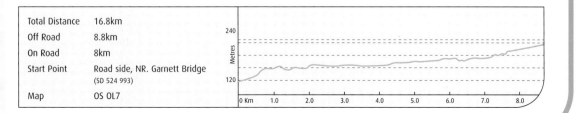

Total Distance	16.8km
Off Road	8.8km
On Road	8km
Start Point	Road side, NR. Garnett Bridge (SD 524 993)
Map	OS OL7

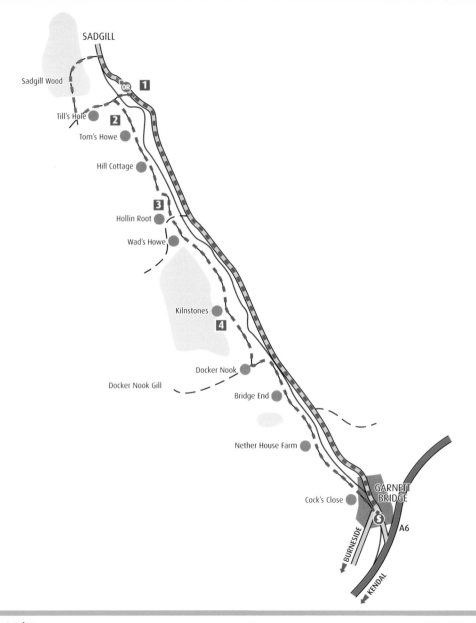

SADGILL

Sadgill Wood

Till's Hole

TOR **1**

2

Tom's Howe

Hill Cottage

3

Hollin Root

Wad's Howe

Kilnstones

4

Docker Nook

Docker Nook Gill

Bridge End

Nether House Farm

Cock's Close

GARNETT BRIDGE

S

A6

BURNESIDE

KENDAL

Route finding is particularly easy on the outward leg. Head back down to the bridge over the River Sprint and turn **L** up the valley. The road climbs steadily for the first km or so, then gently undulates along the valley floor for the next 8km, passing numerous farms and tackling a number of modest climbs and descents until reaching the head of the valley at Sadgill.

1 Before reaching Sadgill, (just past Stockdale bridge) a clearly signposted bridleway goes off to the **L** at Till's Hole Farm.

Take this bridleway (to Till's Hole, and eventually Kentmere). Ride up until you cross the high-sided, concrete bridge over the river, but do not continue up as far as the farm buildings. Immediately after the bridge, you will see a track going off to the **L** and a gate giving access to a lane. (This is the point where the optional route joins up again and is the start of the bridleway back down the valley.)

Optional Route: However, having come all this way, it would be a shame not to carry on the last km to the end of the tarmac road at Sadgill where, from the pretty packhorse bridge, the views up Gatescarth Pass to Buckbarrow Crag are spectacular.

From Sadgill, turn **L,** crossing the bridge onto a bridleway/byway that circles back onto our return route at Till's Hole. This optional route begins behind the farm buildings to climb steadily past Sadgill Wood and through a number of gates. The track steepens and becomes very rocky approaching a higher gate. Once through this gate, **Ignore** the byway branching off to the right over to Kentmere. Instead, take the bridleway **L**, back to Till's Hole, crossing a small stream and then levelling out with fine views behind. After a short distance, turn off **L**,

through a gate, dropping steeply down a grassy field back into the valley and following a number of posts carrying bridleway waymarks, to meet the same stream you crossed a little higher up the hill. If you miss the gate, you will find yourself climbing further up and out of the valley. Once across the stream, follow the wall steeply downwards to the farm at Till's Hole. Cycle straight through the farmyard to where a very high-sided, concrete bridge crosses the river but do not cross it! The bridleway back down the valley goes through the gate on the **R** before reaching the bridge, meeting up with the first route option as it does so.

Essentially, the optional route climbs the (rather steep) hill just to drop back down again. In many respects, the climb is worth doing just for the views it affords of the valley. If however, pushing your bike up a rocky track is not your idea of a fun afternoon, take the first, and considerably easier route back down the valley.

2 The bridleway now gives few route finding problems as it runs parallel to the river, back down towards Garnett Bridge. (If in doubt, keep roughly **SA** on the track and remember that the majority of the tracks off to the **L** will take you back to the road along the valley bottom.)

The track runs alongside the river for a little way before going through a gate onto a concrete farm road. Turn left down the road as far as a cattle grid a little way ahead.

Do not cross the cattle grid but turn **R** through gates to pass in front of farm buildings at Hill Cottage. Continue past a ruined building along the clearly defined track, crossing fields, a wooden bridge and then a small stream onto another track.

3 Follow this easy track to the next farm and climb a short, steep section up to two gates side by side. The left-hand gate is marked private so take the **RH** gateway (the gate itself is missing). Climb a little and then drop down behind the buildings to join the farm access road.

The next farm along is Hollin Root. The main farm access track (left) is also a bridleway which can be followed out to the valley road if you wish. Our bridleway down the valley takes the higher gate on the **R** just in front of the farmhouse onto a pleasant track leading to the next farm at Wad's Howe. A gate leads out onto the farm access drive and our route turns **R** (uphill) in front of the farm and round into the farmyard. Head over towards the

large wooden shed to find the bridleway going off to the **L** through a gate onto a lane. More gates lead into open fields with bridges over small streams. St Mary's Church can be seen ahead on the left at this point as your route heads towards the obvious trees ahead.

Passing through a gate, the obvious track keeps to the **L** of the old hedge, alongside the river. This track can be followed as it swings round to the **R**, and then climbs the rise in front of the farm buildings ahead. However, the track is often flooded and can be very boggy. An easier way to the same place is to pass through the gate then climb the small rise on the **R** as soon as it is convenient. Once on top of the hill, the way forward can be seen, passing through a marked gate to the **R** of the farm buildings ahead. Follow the bridleway signs through a further gate into open fields again, and then aim for the obvious row of trees on the **R**, up on the rise ahead. The track is very easy to follow, as it swings round to a farm at Kilnstones.

4 Do not follow the farm drive but continue directly in front of the house, keeping close to the wall on the **R**, over a slab bridge and through a gate onto a lane.

The lane is very easy to follow and eventually breaks out into a more open area near Docker Nook Farm (the farm is a little over to the right as you look across the field ahead). It is tempting to follow the obvious fence on your left, but technically, the bridleway goes diagonally **R** across the field to a fingerpost in the distance. From the fingerpost, turn **L** down the farm drive, through a gate and continue down the drive. Just as it appears that you are heading out onto the road, turn **R** across a stone slab bridge over the stream and go through a gate into a large, open field. The gate is signposted with a bridleway sign and the track goes **R** across the middle of the boggy field, aiming for the white farm buildings in the distance.

NB If your legs are tired and your bum is too sore to carry on, the farm track out to the road is also classed as a bridleway so you could head onto the tarmac and return down to Garnett Bridge this way if you so desired.

We however, are not wimps, so across the field we go to the distant farmstead of Bridge End. Pass through the two farm gates into the yard and follow the obvious farm track up a steep rise to the clump of trees on top of the hill ahead.

5 A pleasant downhill follows on a good track, through three gates, to break out into the farmyard of Nether House farm. Continue down the farm drive as far as the bridge over the river **but do not cross**. A few yards back, a gate on the **R** is signposted with a slate bridleway sign – this is the way onwards. Follow a good track, up a small rise and through another gate into a large open field. Follow the wall on the **R**, ignoring the first gate and continue to the end of the field where two gates will be found side by side. Take the **RH** gate into the next field and aim for the lowest point of the small rise ahead of you. Once on top of the rise, the gate in the bottom of the field can be seen, along with views of a small tarn just ahead. Through the gate, keep to the **L** of the tarn then drop down to the **R** right corner of the field, where an obvious gap in the wall (with a signpost) allows access to a continuation of the track. Follow it first to the **L** then back **R** to climb a small rise, keeping to the **R** of an old hedge. The track quickly reaches the final gate of the route before continuing down the narrow lane ahead to pop out between the houses in Garnett Bridge just next to the river.

settle, feizor
& wharfe

ROUTE 7 // 12km (7.5 miLes)

A lovely and highly recommended route giving spectacular views over Ingleborough and Pen-y-ghent with surprisingly gentle climbing on excellent trails. Wharfe and Feizor are charming Dales villages but not so large or well known as to tempt many visitors off the main roads. What better way could there be of exploring the true essence of Dales country life than to ride along a secluded bridleway into the heart of an unspoiled hamlet? The route includes a section of the new Pennine Bridleway as it passes through this fabulous limestone scenery.

To begin, find the B6480 running north-west out of Settle (hint: it's the main road). You're either going to have to drive or cycle up it to get to the start of the route proper, so choose now. If you decide to start in Settle be aware that the B6480 climbs up through Giggleswick and then up and up, (and up again) alongside Giggleswick Scar to Scar Top Garage.

Being an essentially slothful character, I prefer to drive up to the top of the scar and park in the convenient layby directly opposite the garage.

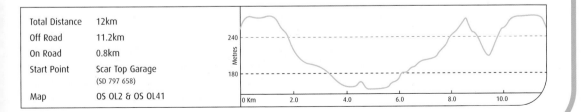

Total Distance	12km
Off Road	11.2km
On Road	0.8km
Start Point	Scar Top Garage (SD 797 658)
Map	OS OL2 & OS OL41

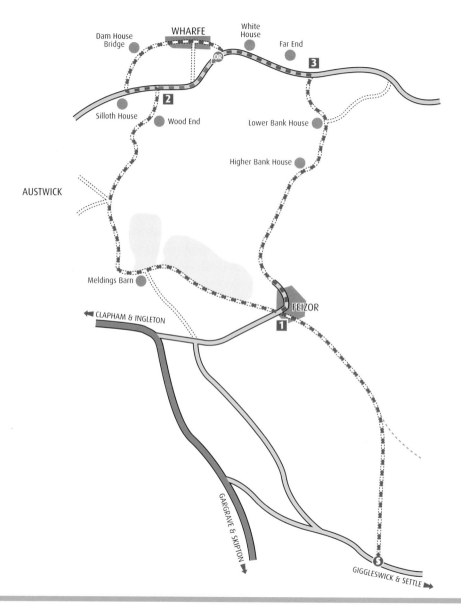

Dam House
Bridge

WHARFE

White
House

Far End

3

OR

Silloth House

2

Wood End

Lower Bank House

Higher Bank House

AUSTWICK

Meldings Barn

FEIZOR

1

◄ CLAPHAM & INGLETON

GARGRAVE & SKIPTON

S

GIGGLESWICK & SETTLE ►

However you chose to get up onto Giggleswick Scar, the route begins through a gate signposted (Bridleway to Feizor) almost directly opposite the house attached to Scar Top Garage, about 20m back down the hill from the layby.

The trail climbs steeply through the limestone scars at first but, although steep, the climb is not very long. After a couple of hundred metres, a track enters from a gate on the left to cross the bridleway at right angles. It is tempting to assume here that the bridleway continues straight ahead at this point but you would be wrong! In fact, the route towards Feizor takes the gate on the **L** then, bearing **R** up an obvious track, climbs the grassy hill. At the next field boundary (and gate) the track can be clearly seen dropping down, alongside a prominent sheepfold, to an equally prominent ladder stile. The more thoughtful of you may therefore question why a bridleway would incorporate a stile to cross a wall but, upon arrival, a partially hidden gate directly alongside will reassure you that you are indeed on the correct bridleway.

Once through the gate, follow the obvious (and very pleasant) track across the next field, aiming for the corner of a wall ahead. From the wall corner, the track becomes more of a lane and passes through the next gate, alongside a sheepfold on the right. Once through the gate, continue to follow the wall on the **L** for a little way until the track bears off to the **R** to a prominent signpost. The signpost (somewhat unhelpfully) only points back along the bridleway in the direction you have just come! (From 'Buck Haw Brow'). However, the track onwards is very clear, dropping down the hill to the little cluster of farms and houses that make up the hamlet of Feizor.

NB. When you reach Feizor, take a good look at the entrance to the bridleway you just dropped out of – you'll be turning up it again later in the ride.

1 Once on the tarmac road in the village, turn **L** then, almost immediately, **R** along a signposted bridleway between farm buildings, on Hale Lane. The track is surfaced at first but then becomes rockier as the farm buildings are left behind. Very pleasant riding along a good track between walls now follows, until a junction is reached at a partially ruined barn (Meldings Barn).

Turn **R** at the barn, along another similar track, to run below Oxenber Wood (which is on your right). After a short distance, a junction of four bridleways is reached. The tracks left and straight ahead drop down into the village of Austwick, where, if you are looking for food or refreshments, you can find a pub and shops.

If however, you are champing at the bit to continue onwards, then your route from the meeting of the four bridleways takes the track behind you and to the **R**, (Wood Lane), which climbs a little before turning sharp **L** to continue rising more gently and then dropping down towards the farm at Wood End. The track doglegs sharp **L** then drops down a small hill to turn back sharp **R** and on into the farmyard. Turn **L** down the farm lane to meet the tarmac road on the outskirts of the village of Wharfe.

2 Three bridleways allow optional routes into the village then back out onto the road. The most pleasant of these can be found by turning **L** down the road for about 200m to Silloth House. Opposite the house, you will find an obvious (and pleasant) bridleway, which crosses Austwick Beck at Dam House Bridge and then climbs gently into the hamlet. **Don't** take the first lane to the right out of the village, but aim **SA**, (eastwards) to find the higher lane back out to the road. On meeting the road turn **L** uphill to climb past White House and Far End farms on your left.

Optional route: If you do not wish to undertake this rather pleasant excursion into Wharfe however, it is possible to turn **R** where the farm track from Wood End meets the road and follow it as it climbs steadily past Wharfe, and on to the farms at White House and Far End.

3 A couple of fields (about 100m) past Far End is the access drive to Lower Bark House on your **R**. Turn up this, following the signposted bridleway, through the farmyard then turn **R** behind the barns to climb steadily up the hill towards Higher Bark House. The track is obvious as it climbs steadily to a gate on the top of the hill.

Go **SA** through the gate, down a very attractive lane dropping, gently at first, and then more steeply, back to the hamlet of Feizor. Follow the tarmac road through the village, looking out for the bridleway on the **L** that you tore down a little earlier in the day on the outward route.

Climb steadily back up the hill to the 'Stackhouse' and 'Buck Haw Brow' signpost. Bear off **R** here, to follow the good trail (unfortunately uphill on the way back!) to the junction just above the road at Scar Top Garage. Turn **R** to drop down the hill to the road and the end of the ride (unless you parked in Settle, in which case you need to turn **L** and roll all the way down into the town).

PHOTO RIGHT // a taste of real mountain biking in the yorkshire dales

ambleside to troutbeck
via robin's lane

route 8 // 11.2km (7 miles)

Driving from valley to valley in the National Park is plagued by the ever-present queues of traffic headed by a Morris Minor driven at 10 miles per hour by some old guy who wonders why they ever did away with the man walking in front with a red flag. This route climbs steeply through Skelghyll Woods from Ambleside, passing Jenkin Crag and some lovely views before descending to the idyllic village of Troutbeck in the next valley. It then winds past the historic farmhouse of Town End before dropping down to the Lake District visitor centre at Brockhole and a return along the edge of Lake Windermere! Good riding with great views – what are you waiting for?

Start the ride from any of the many car parks in and around Ambleside, and then head for the large garden centre (Hayes) on the A591 at Waterhead. Almost immediately opposite the garden centre is a pay and display car park, complete with public toilets and a small shop. The ride description will start from this conveniently sited car park.

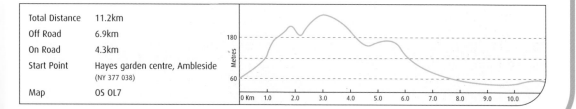

Total Distance	11.2km
Off Road	6.9km
On Road	4.3km
Start Point	Hayes garden centre, Ambleside (NY 377 038)
Map	OS OL7

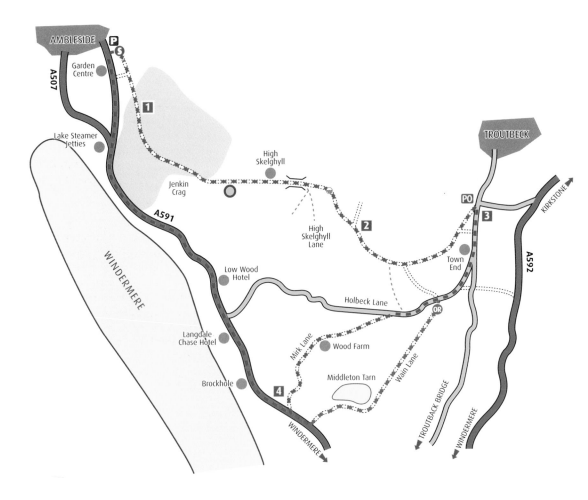

AMBLESIDE

P
S

A507

Garden
Centre

Lake Steamer
Jetties

1

Jenkin
Crag

A591

High
Skelghyll

High
Skelghyll
Lane

2

WINDERMERE

Low Wood
Hotel

Holbeck Lane

Langdale
Chase Hotel

Milk Lane

Wood Farm

Brockhole

4

Middleton Tarn

Wain Lane

WINDERMERE

TROUTBECK

KIRKSTONE

PO

3

Town
End

A592

OR

TROUTBACK BRIDGE

WINDERMERE

At the rear of the car park (furthest away from the A591) is a small minor road running parallel to the main road. Turn **R** along this but watch almost immediately for an even narrower lane going off **L** and heading steeply uphill. The lane is clearly signposted to Skelghyll Woods and Jenkins Crag. If you meet the main A591, you will know that you have gone too far and missed the narrow lane.

Brace yourself at this point for a steep and constant climb for about 1km! Luckily, there are a number of attractive viewpoints along the way which will give you a plausible excuse to stop and gaze at the view whilst allowing your lungs to recover and your heart rate to drop to a level that sustains human life. Don't be put off by the climb, the scenery is very pleasant (particularly on the top) and the views down Windermere are well worth the effort.

Route finding is never really a problem on the way up. There are a number of private drives branching off to big, posh houses, but these are invariably signposted as being private and there is a profusion of helpful signs pointing ever-upwards to Skelghyll Woods and Jenkins Crag – four of them at one junction! Once in the woods, there is one junction of paths which may cause a little confusion because the main path (to the **L**) carries a National Trust sign describing it as a 'footpath' to Troutbeck. You will be glad to know that the sign is quite wrong and that the path (which you need to take) is indeed a bridleway. Apart from that, follow the signs and you won't go wrong.

1 Once in the woods, the tarmac lane gives way to a pleasant, unsurfaced track which generally allows good riding with the occasional rocky section requiring a push. The route keeps climbing steadily, all the way through the wooded area, with tantalising glimpses of views down the valley to Windermere. At a particularly rocky section alongside a stream, a path goes off to the left but **ignore this**, cross the stream by means of a small bridge and follow the main track up the **RH** side of the beck. Finally, the wooded area to your right opens out onto fields with views to die for. Rest awhile here, (they have even provided benches to rest your aching limbs) and be content in the knowledge that the hard work is now largely over.

The lane now gives easy riding, in lovely situations, to reach a small farm at High Skelghyll. Drop down through the farmyard and continue to run down the farm drive as far as a bridge over a small stream (Holbeck Ghyll). **Stop at the bridge** however, for the obvious continuation of the farm track ahead is only classed as a footpath and is clearly marked as such! Instead, your route goes through the gate on the **L** to zigzag up a small hill, past a ruined barn, to a junction with a larger lane (Robin Lane).

2 Turn **R** downhill and begin your exhilarating descent down into Troutbeck. During the descent, you will see a footpath and two bridleways heading off to your right. It is possible to use either of the bridleways as optional routes down to the road but Robin Lane is longer, downhill, easily rideable and therefore much more fun. If you do opt to take one of the two bridleways, skip straight to direction **3**

Robin Lane becomes a tarmac road at a few cottages just above the main village. Continue down the lane to meet the main road through the village at the Post Office.

3 Turn **R** along the busier road, to pass the National Trust property of Town End Farm and take the first minor road that branches off uphill to the **R**.

Climb gently away from the village, **ignoring the first two bridleways** on the **L**. As the top of the hill is approached, an obvious bridleway joins the road on the right. This is one of the optional bridleways you could have used to drop down from Robin Lane. A few yards further on, another bridleway goes off **L** at a bend in the road.

Optional route: Take this bridleway (which is signposted and displays prominent warning signs prohibiting motorcycles from using the track). This is Wain Lane and is one of the two possible descent routes down to the road alongside Lake Windermere. The lane is easy to follow but is extremely rocky, (and even unrideable) in places. If you do decide to take this option, the riding becomes more pleasant as the lane skirts round Middlerigg Tarn to meet the A591 just below the Lake District National Park Centre at Brockhole.

To find the recommended descent from the top of the hill at Troutbeck, ignore Wain Lane going off **L** and continue along the minor road ahead (Holbeck Lane). A short distance further along, at a farm on the **L**, another bridleway (the charmingly named Mirk Lane) drops down the hill to the **L**, through the farm buildings. Mirk Lane is used to access fields further down the hill and gives a much more pleasant ride. The track is very easy to follow through a number of gates, until it drops onto the tarmac drive of a large house on the right (Wood Farm).

The obvious temptation at this point is to shoot off down the very inviting driveway ahead, but stop! On the **R**, immediately past the garden area of the house, an easily missed footpath sign indicates the true route onwards. Hidden in the undergrowth here is an even smaller and more easily missed bridleway sign which reinforces this fact. The track runs directly in front of the house and then climbs gently up through Newclose Wood. Follow this track as it drops downhill again, to emerge onto the A591 just a little nearer the visitor centre at Brockhole than the Wain Lane route.

4 From here, regardless of which descent route you took, turn **R** along the A591 and follow the clearly marked cycleway to return along the side of the lake to Ambleside and your transport.

Optional finish: Mirk Lane emerges onto the A591 directly opposite the entrance to the Lake District National Park Visitor Centre at Brockhole. One of the amenities offered at Brockhole is a jetty which allows the Windermere Steamers to pick up passengers. This useful facility allows tired cyclists to spend a little time exploring Brockhole then to wander off down to the jetty and catch the steamer up the lake to Ambleside - a very civilised (if somewhat indolent) alternative end to your ride.

pelter bridge
& Loughrigg terrace

route 9 // 8.8km (5.5 miles)

A lovely little route, roughly two thirds of which is off-road on some great tracks. Popular with mountain bikers, yet not so technically difficult as to be unrideable for the majority of riders, this is a good choice for those who prefer to have dirt, rather than tarmac, under their tyres.

Leaving Pelter Bridge, the route follows a quiet lane alongside the River Rothay to the outskirts of Ambleside, where it climbs steeply onto Loughrigg Fell. Fun rocky tracks lead over the top of the fell and down to the tarn on the other side, from where more lanes lead towards Loughrigg Terrace. The terrace itself gives a lovely downhill glide in a wonderful setting before disappearing beneath the surface or Rydal Water...

On the outskirts of Ambleside, 4km along the main A591 to Keswick, but before reaching Wordsworth's house at Rydal Mount, turn **L** over the quaint little Pelter Bridge (crossing the River Rothay). Immediately over the bridge, turn **R** to find a convenient car park which forms the starting point for this ride.

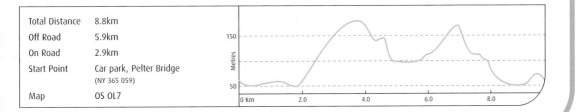

Total Distance	8.8km	
Off Road	5.9km	
On Road	2.9km	
Start Point	Car park, Pelter Bridge (NY 365 059)	
Map	OS OL7	

photo // rydal water from Loughrigg terrace

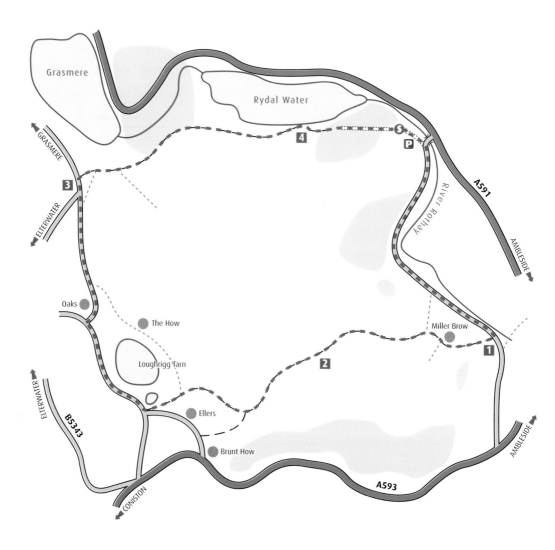

Grasmere

Rydal Water

GRASMERE

ELTERWATER

3

River Rothay

A591

AMBLESIDE

4

5

P

Oaks

The How

Miller Brow

2

1

Loughrigg Tarn

ELTERWATER

B5343

Ellers

Brunt How

AMBLESIDE

CONISTON

A593

Lakes & Dales

From the car park, ride back down towards the bridge but **do not cross it**. Instead, turn **R** down the quiet tarmac road back towards Ambleside with the River Rothay flowing serenely through water meadows on your left. After about 2½km, and just before reaching the footbridge over to Rothay Park near Ambleside, a lane climbs steeply off to the **R** over a cattle grid. Sadly, this hill is our way forward. (You knew it was going to be upwards, didn't you?)

1 Climb up the hill, past a number of houses to where a gate is met and woodland gives way to open fell on the left-hand side of the track. Unfortunately, the climbing is still not quite over yet (but the situation is very pleasant and, let's be honest, if you weren't here you would only be at home sitting with your feet up watching rubbish on the telly). So breathe deeply, feel those muscles pounding and climb more easily now, **SA** along the bridleway through another two gates and on to the open fell-side at the top of the hill.

Route finding is very easy on this ride and your trail can be seen ahead, dropping steadily downward around the flank of the hill towards Loughrigg Tarn, way off in the distance. The riding is fast, easy and great fun, but show a little caution as the trail is narrow and rocky in places. I well remember glancing back to see how far I had left the others behind, only to look forwards again just in time to see my front wheel drop casually off the track and into the ditch. The resulting double somersault with half-twist was quite spectacular (or so they told me 15 minutes later when they had finally managed to stop laughing).

2 As you drop down this excellent track, a gate will be found passing through the wall on the left, alongside a small sheepfold. This is a bridleway which drops steeply down to a farm between Ellers and Brunt How. **Ignore this** and keep to the main track as it winds gently downwards and to the **R**, around the flank of the hill.

Approaching the bottom of the hill, the trail goes through a gate into woodland and then drops down a tricky, rocky section to break out quickly at a junction with a large gate on the right and a cluster of houses ahead.

3 The aforementioned gate clearly states that no cycling is allowed along the road past a house called The How. Instead, follow the road **SA**, past the cottages at Tarn Foot and almost immediately, out onto the quiet road at Little Loughrigg. Turn **R** along this road, enjoying views of the Tarn over the wall on the right, until you meet a Y-junction a little further along.

Bear **R** at this junction, (towards Grasmere), past a farmstead called 'Oaks' and climb steadily up Red Bank until it just begins to drop down the other side towards Grasmere. Ignore the first footpath sign on the right but take the bridleway, also on the **R**, soon afterwards. This is the start of Loughrigg Terrace, a superb descent which amply makes up for all the sweat expended in getting up here in the first place. The views over Grasmere are fantastic but make sure you watch the path as well as the scenery – there are some tricky little rocky sections waiting to trap the unwary!

4 The trail is very obvious with one particularly rocky section, where a footpath comes out of Baneriggs Wood on the left. Continue down to Rydal Water and ride along its shore until you cross a small wooden bridge and come to a halt looking a little bemused. Unless the weather has been particularly dry for a long time, (unlikely in the Lake District) your track looks as though it disappears into the lake – and you would be right! Cycle moistly around the rocky outcrop to arrive, somewhat damper, on the other side and at the continuation of the bridleway, which climbs briefly up to a gate and into a walled lane, that leads quickly back to the car park at Pelter Bridge.

KINGSDALE

ROUTE 10 // 11.6km (7.2 miles)

Kingsdale is an area steeped in history. The whole valley was once covered by an ancient lake before the water broke through the glacial dam at the southern end and left a classic glacial profile. Later habitation then filled Kingsdale with the remains of early Viking settlers. More recently still, Kingsdale has become the haunt of the caving fraternity and some of the classic potholes of Britain can be found in this area.

This route follows the very quiet road up the valley (lovely dry stone walls) and then climbs off-road up to the Turbary Road; an ancient track once used to bring fuel down from the higher fells. The Turbary Road runs back parallel with the road over a pleasant grassy surface and the views (as far as Morecambe Bay!) from its position high in the valley are well worth the effort put in getting up there. At one point, high above the valley, you'll hear the sound of rushing water where no stream can be seen. Will the rocky crevasse to your left reveal the answer?

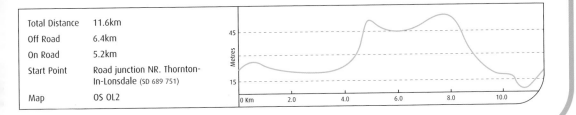

Total Distance	11.6km
Off Road	6.4km
On Road	5.2km
Start Point	Road junction NR. Thornton-In-Lonsdale (SD 689 751)
Map	OS OL2

PHOTO // TRICKY CLIMBING

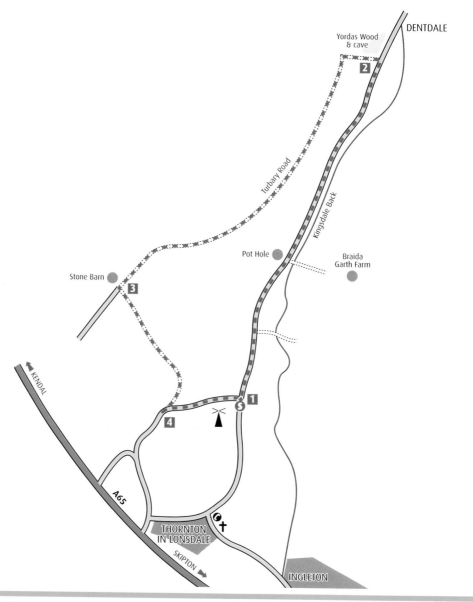

DENTDALE

Yordas Wood & cave

2

Turbary Road

Kingsdale Back

Pot Hole

Braida Garth Farm

Stone Barn

3

KENDAL

4

S **1**

A65

THORNTON IN LONSDALE

SKIPTON ►

INGLETON

Thornton in Lonsdale is a small hamlet less than a couple of km out of Ingleton. It boasts an excellent pub, a picturesque church, (where Arthur Conan Doyle was married) a caravan park and a cluster of houses. This route can be started from the village but the climb up to Kingsdale itself is both steep and everlasting! Personally, I prefer to drive up to the top and start the ride from there. Either way, whether by car or by bike, if you stand with the church on your right and the Marton Arms on your left, the road to Kingsdale (and then over into Dentdale) is the minor road which goes off **R** at the telephone box. Passing the village stocks by the churchyard, the road climbs steeply until, almost on the top of the hill, a minor road joins from the left, near a large telecommunications mast.

There is ample parking near this junction if you choose to drive up from Thornton-on-Lonsdale and your return route will see you puffing and panting up this minor road back to the car – and then back down to the pub no doubt!

1 Follow the main road up the valley as it first climbs a little then drops steeply back down with fantastic views along the length of Kingsdale. Ignore the bridleway on the right at the bottom of the hill. This crosses the river and heads off into Twisleton and Chapel-le-Dale. The main valley road keeps close to the stream, climbing very gently past the drive to Braida Garth Farm. There will usually be lots of cavers' cars parked in this area and a peer over the wall on your left will reveal a lidded oil drum buried in the hillside. This is the lower (valley entrance) to the Kingsdale Master Cave system and your ride will pass a number of the other entrances on the return leg, much higher up the hillside.

Continue up the valley, along pleasant, undulating terrain that rises gently along the whole length of the valley. After about 4km, a short steep hill with obvious parking areas on both sides and a copse of trees (Yordas Wood) on the **L** marks the position of Yordas Cave. If you miss this point, you will shortly reach the next (the only other) farm in the valley and will realise that you have gone too far.

2 At Yordas wood, go through the gate on the **L** of the road at the base of the short hill. The obvious track climbs directly up to the wood but this is the cavers' path up to the cave system. You are looking for the indistinct track that climbs the hill ahead but to the **L** of the wood.

Digression

Yordas Cave was once a Victorian show cave, which ladies in crinoline dresses would visit for a taste of adventure. The entrance has a few steps going down into a huge chamber, which can easily be explored if you happen to bring a torch with you. In all but very wet conditions, the active stream sinks in the floor of the chamber allowing easy exploration up towards the sound of a waterfall at the far end. The waterfall splashes down impressively into a small chamber from a number of higher entrances. This is as far as your visit can be taken, so retrace your steps back to the entrance and start hauling yourself and your bike up the hill to the high-level track.

This is the strenuous section of the trip as the track climbs up the hill, bearing slightly **L**. After the first steep section, the track disappears but it can be spotted ahead, veering back **R** towards the top of Yordas Wood. From here, the track is quite clear, heading straight upwards, parallel to the stream and with the wall on your **R**. Continue upwards to the top **RH** corner of the field where a gate through the wall allows access to the Turbary Road proper. The gate is very prominent as it has an impressive pile of limestone boulders blocking access, presumably to stop motor vehicles from churning up the track.

The tough climb now over, turn **L** the Turbary Road is a little boggy and indistinct to begin with but soon gives very pleasant riding along a grassy plateau on the lower flanks of Gragareth. Unfortunately, the four-wheel drive enthusiasts sometimes churn up the surface in odd places, giving a more 'entertaining' ride. Cave systems abound on both sides of this track but please be cautious. All of the entrances finish up in the Master Cave (lower than road level) and most drop down very impressive shafts to get there. Jingling Pot on the right of the track (marked by a solitary tree) and Rowten Pot, (the impressive cleft a little further along on the left) are particularly impressive but unforgiving. A slip down either of these would not be good for your longevity!

The Turbary Road continues along a good, grassy surface through a number of gates until it begins to drop downhill and becomes a rocky track. Through more gates, the track becomes even more rocky and uneven approaching a reservoir pumping station on the right (a stone barn). At this point, the track meets the tarmac road coming up from the village of Masongill.

3 Do not continue onto the tarmac, but take the excellent track heading off to the **L**. (Tow Scar Road) Fine, downhill riding passes through more gates and a short uphill section. The track once more drops downwards to meet another tarmac road with a farm on the right. (Westgate)

4 This road is the one leading upwards, past the telecommunications tower back to your car, so follow it to the **L** as it rises steadily to a well-earned rest.

If you were brave enough to begin this ride from the pub, then a more gentle way back would be to turn **R** onto the tarmac road, past Westgate farm then take the first lane off to the **L**. This lane drops down to a T-junction where a further **L** turn will bring you back into the village and your car.

KIRKBY LONSDALE
to MANSERGH

ROUTE 11 // 16km (10 miles)

Kirkby Lonsdale is well known to the tourist throngs who flock to this very attractive market town during the summer season. A short ride away from the town itself, a host of traffic-free lanes, tracks and bridleways can be combined to provide an excellent ride. This route links up the best of these lanes and tracks to give a very pleasant outing, far away from the hustle and bustle of the tourist hotspots all around. The views over to Barbondale from this ride are spectacular and well worth the effort spent in getting there.

There is a special feel about this route because the bridleways around this area have not been heavily used; they are how bridleways ought to be – ancient hedgerows, mixed woodland and farm lanes. This is country riding at its best, these lanes and tracks have changed so little over the years that you could almost expect a hay-wain to come trundling around the corner at any time. A ride not to be missed!

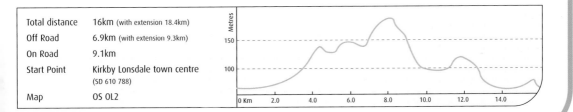

Total distance	16km (with extension 18.4km)	
Off Road	6.9km (with extension 9.3km)	
On Road	9.1km	
Start Point	Kirkby Lonsdale town centre (SD 610 788)	
Map	OS OL2	

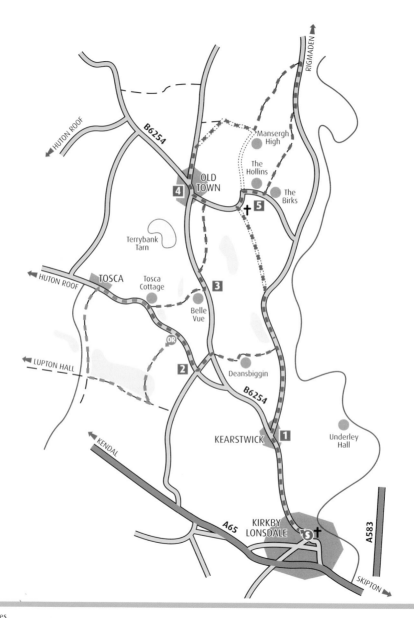

Lakes & Dales

From the church in Kirkby Lonsdale, take the B6254 away from the town centre and up a short hill, in the direction of Kendal. The road quickly leaves the houses behind as it passes signs for the rugby club and then an unusually ornate lodge house from the Underley Hall Estate. A little further along the road, a few houses are met at the hamlet of Kearstwick, a kilometre or so out of Kirkby Lonsdale, and a road goes off to the **R**, signposted Rigmaden and Killington.

1 Take this **R** turn and head gently uphill past the entrance to Underley Hall School and a plantation on the right. After 1km and just before a house called Scar Brow, a bridleway goes off **L** along a drive to Deansbiggin. Follow this through the farmyard and along a pleasant track through a wood, to emerge on the B6254 again. Turn **R** along the road and climb a short distance to a junction with the first minor road on the left. Take the **L** turn at this junction and climb up to a crossroads.

2 Turn **R** at the crossroads and continue to climb up the hill ahead. After 1km, a signposted bridleway goes off to the left. This bridleway is the optional off-road extension to the route (see the end of the route for directions), which adds about 2½km to the total distance. Route finding on this extension is relatively easy, although the riding is mainly across hilly fields and can be tiring in places. A description of this optional section is given at the end of the main route description.

If you decide to reject the extension, continue **SA** up the minor road, past one plantation on the right and another on the left, to arrive at Tosca Cottage (on the right-hand side of the road) after another 500m.

Immediately before Tosca Cottage, a bridleway goes off **R**. (This is where the optional route re-joins the main ride). Take this bridleway through the gate, **ignoring a prominent track going off to the left**, across a field and through a gate in the far wall. The correct route heads **SA** to the left of the obvious copse of trees. Head uphill, through two gates, to another small copse on the brow of the small rise ahead. As you reach the copse, the track goes between a wall and some trees to enter a short section of lane and a gate.

Immediately through this gate, the bridleway should (i.e. on the map) bear left across the field towards Belle Vue Farm, just ahead. A modern fence prevents this, so follow the farm track **SA**, down to the farm, and then round to the **L** in front of the farmhouse, to the two corrugated barns. Follow the obvious track, between the two barns, then down the main farm drive to join the B6254 again.

3 Turn **L** along the B6254 and begin the climb up the hill ahead. After a short distance (about 200m), a farm gate on the right is passed and, just after it, a signposted bridleway goes off to the **R** near Stoneriggs Wood. Take this bridleway and follow it along a bumpy track, between hedges, to the farm at Hawkrigg. Follow the concrete drive through the farm buildings and out to a minor road just down the hill from Old Town. Turn **L** here, up the road, to meet again our old friend the B6254 at a T-junction in the village.

4 Turn **R** onto the B6254 then, almost immediately, another minor road goes off to the **R** and this should be followed up to a farm at Mireside. Immediately after the farm, a tarmac lane goes off steeply to the **R**. Follow this lane, past a group of industrial buildings on the left. This short climb is well worth the effort because the views across the valley to Barbondale are fantastic. The road climbs on a little further, past Town Head on the right, to a sharp **RH** bend at the top of the hill. **Ignore** the bridleway going off sharp left here, and take the **R** turn to drop down a fast, steep descent to Mansergh High at the bottom of the hill.

Turn **L** along a short length of lane which stops at a farm gate, with a bridleway sign through a smaller gate on the left. The bridleway is very overgrown and many users continue through the farm gate to a well-defined track alongside the hedge on the left, (immediately alongside the bridleway), to a point where it merges with the bridleway. Technically, you should follow the bridleway until you pass a barn on the right and a gate, opening into the next field. Cross this field to another gate opening into a much larger field.

The route heads diagonally **R** (downhill) here, to a gate in the opposite corner, near an old disused cottage. Pass the cottage, enter a wood and follow the obvious path downhill, through attractive woodland, to a gate overlooking the grounds of Rigmaden Park and the impressive Hall itself (a little way off on the other side of the road). The track now leaves the wood to run downhill, across the field ahead, following an excellent track to meet the road at a gate.

Turn **R** along the road for 600m, past a small plantation on the left until, at the far end of the trees, a bridleway will be found going off to the **R**. Take this bridleway, which is very easy to follow and on excellent tracks. Pass through a number of gates and, just beyond a stream and gate, climb a short rise to meet a minor road between farms at The Hollins and The Birks.

5 Turn **R** along this road and follow it past The Hollins and around a sharp **LH** bend to drop down to a large parking area at Mansergh church hall. Keep to the **L** in front of the hall and take the tarmac lane that climbs up to the church. The tarmac stops at the church gate but the lane continues through a gate into open fields. The track (Chapel Lane) runs pleasantly alongside hedges on the right, then between hedgerows, to drop down to a minor road at Mansergh Hall. Turn **R** here, to follow the road, firstly uphill, then down past the house at Scar Brow on the left.

You should soon recognise this road as the one you wheezed up at the start of your ride a little while ago. Follow it down, past the entrance to Underley School again, to the main road at Kearstwick. Turn **L** here, following the B6254 back to Kirkby Lonsdale in just under 2km.

Optional Route: Climbing up the hill from the crossroads, at **2** a bridleway sign is met on the **L**. Take this bridleway, through the gate into a field and follow the wall on the **L** along a clearly defined track, aiming for the very large barn in the next field. Just before the barn, a gate gives access through the field wall.

Aim slightly uphill to pass just behind the barn (which is in a sad state of disrepair) and follow the fence line on your right. Just past the barn, the fence begins to drop downhill to an unusually shaped metal gate giving access to the large plantation ahead. The track is very easy to spot as it turns slightly **L** and drops down the hill.

Squelch through a boggy section in the hollow to arrive quickly at a crossroads with a very well-defined farm track running through the wood. Turn **L** along this track, where pleasant riding will bring you to the edge of the wood at a farm gate.

Do not follow the track through the gate ahead, but instead, go through an alternative gate on the **R**. From this point, the bridleway essentially follows the boundary wall of the plantation (which is on your **R**). However, you will first need to cross the small stream at the bottom of the small hill ahead of you. Pick your own route down the hill and either tiptoe hesitantly, or wade fearlessly, across the beck. Once this damp obstacle is behind you, climb up the rise on the other side aiming for the plantation boundary wall on your **R**.

The plantation is situated on a hill, so head upwards, still following the boundary wall, with nice views on the left over to Lupton and Farleton. Once on the top of the hill, a fun descent runs down the other side, through one gate and down a steeper section to a crossing of tracks at the far corner of the plantation.

Ignore the track going straight ahead (to Lupton) and the track going left (to Fleet and Spital). Our route follows the edge of the plantation again by turning **R** at the junction and passing immediately through a gate. Once through the gate, a boggy, fenced area prevents you from keeping close to the wood, but a short detour around this small obstacle allows you to pick up an obvious track. This track follows the wood for a short distance then veers across the field to the **L**, aiming for a gate near the small copse on the other side, as Lupton Beck is met. This is a pretty spot and the area around the beck would be perfect for a picnic stop if you remembered to bring your sandwiches with you.

The bridleway now follows the beck upstream around the base of Tosca Hill. The track is indistinct in places but generally follows the line of least resistance on the lower ground, alongside the stream. Eventually, the stream meanders round to meet the hill and forces a climb up a short slope onto higher ground. Once on top, continue to follow roughly the direction of the stream until the buildings of Tosca Farm come into view just ahead. Aim for the buildings, where a gate allows access onto a minor road just at the entrance to this attractive farm.

Turn **R** along the road and, after a few hundred metres, Tosca Cottage is met on the left. Just after the cottage, a bridleway is signposted going through a gate on the **L** of the road and you need to turn **L**, re-joining the main route.

cLaife HeiGHts

ROUTE 12 // 12.8km (8 miLes)

Looking out across Windermere from Bowness, the imposing, tree-covered hill on the far shore is Claife Heights. This lovely route follows the western edge of Windermere along some easy tracks (it shares the first couple of km with the Bowness to Ambleside route) **before climbing steeply onto the hilltop for some excellent tracks and fantastic views over the higher fells, before a cracking descent back to Windermere. This area is justly popular with mountain bikers, but the riding is never unduly difficult. Another route you will want to repeat again and again!**

You have two starting options. You can start the ride from any of the many car parks in and around Bowness then cycle down to the Steamer jetty area known as the Glebe, catching the Windermere Car Ferry, which docks 1km to the south of the pedestrian ferries in Bowness, over to the western side of the lake. Alternatively, you can make the longish drive around the lake and park near to where the ferry docks – there is a car park at Station Scar Wood (SD 388 960) which is actually on the route of the cycle track. It's your choice!

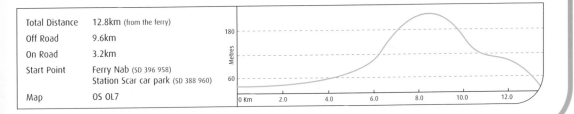

Total Distance	12.8km (from the ferry)
Off Road	9.6km
On Road	3.2km
Start Point	Ferry Nab (SD 396 958) Station Scar car park (SD 388 960)
Map	OS OL7

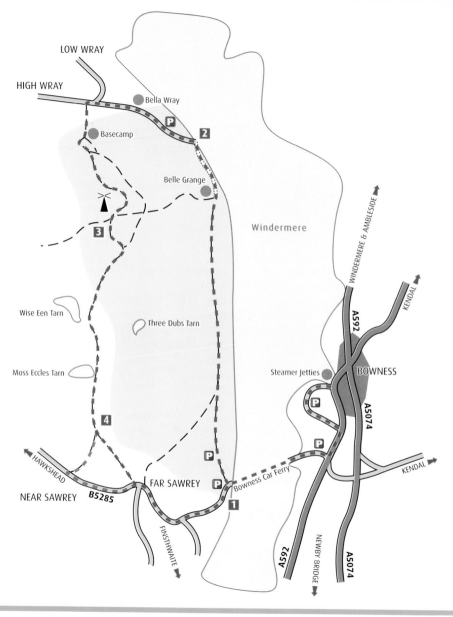

LOW WRAY

HIGH WRAY

Bella Wray

P

2

Basecamp

Belle Grange

3

Windermere

Wise Een Tarn

Three Dubs Tarn

Moss Eccles Tarn

4

HAWKSHEAD

FAR SAWREY

NEAR SAWREY

B5285

P

P

Bowness Car Ferry

1

FINSTHWAITE

A592

NEWBY BRIDGE

Steamer Jetties

BOWNESS

P

A592

P

WINDERMERE & AMBLESIDE

KENDAL

A5074

KENDAL

A5074

From the steamer jetties, the main road (A592) can be followed directly out of Bowness towards Newby Bridge and the Windermere Car Ferry. Alternatively, a small road leads off to the **R** along the edge of the lake, past numerous shops, ice cream parlours and boat houses to turn **R** where it rejoins the A592 a little further along towards the ferry. Turn **R** onto the B5285, just before the marina, following the signs to the car ferry, to join the inevitable queue of cars. Fortunately, a bike does not count as a car, so cycle serenely past the waiting hordes to the head of the queue and enjoy your trip across the lake to the other side.

If you opted out of the ferry trip, make your way to the western landing stage and follow the directions from this point.

1 From the opposite landing stage, the road winds first **L** then back **R** around a small headland. After a short distance, turn **R** at a sharp **LH** bend, onto a narrow, tarmac lane. Follow this as it runs through woodland, then into more open terrain in a very attractive situation with the lake on your right.

Eventually the tarmac runs out and you continue **SA** onto a well-graded (if sometimes muddy) track that continues to run alongside the lake for about 3km. Ignore the occasional bridleway which climbs off to the left up onto Claife Heights.

Eventually, a smoother, gravel surface is reached through a gate at the drive to Belle Grange. Ignoring the bridleway on the left, ride **SA** along the gravel lane until you hit tarmac and begin to rise more steeply.

2 Follow the tarmac road uphill, (**don't** take the bridleway off to the right at the car park), climbing steadily past Balla Wray and on to the cluster of houses at High Wray. At the road junction, keep to the **L**, along the road signposted to Hawkshead.

After a very short distance, (50m, just past a house called Brow Foot) a good, gravel lane goes off uphill, to your left, signposted for 'Basecamp'. I'm sorry to say that this track climbs steeply upwards, (you had guessed that it probably would, hadn't you!) until a junction is met in a wooded area, with wood cabins in the trees to your left.

Here, there is a choice of a low route or a high route. Your route onwards is, of course, the uphill route, past the barrier on your right and up the permissive bridleway beyond (the barrier is only there to stop motor vehicles).

The climbing becomes steadily less severe, but it still tends to be more upwards than downwards until a Y-junction is met. One track drops downhill to the left, whilst you need to take the **RH** branch, along a level track which disappears round a corner bearing rightwards. Follow it round the corner and discover, to your dismay, that it starts to climb again. Don't worry though, the top is nearly in sight and you have the downhill bit to come!

The top is finally reached at an open area called 'Guide Post' and is clearly distinguished by the... well... the guide post actually!

3 To the right a bridleway climbs even further upwards and is signposted to Hawkshead. This should be ignored. To the left (downhill) is a bridleway to Belle Grange, which you passed earlier in the day down on the lakeside. This should also be ignored. A process of elimination discounts the route you just took up and therefore, the only choice left open to you is the very sensible bridleway **SA**, signed Ferry and Far Sawrey. Even better, this excellent track is downhill: what a refreshing change!

The downhill run soon gives way to another short section of uphill, until another crossroads is reached where the route straight ahead is not available to you because it is shown as a footpath. Turn **R** here, uphill, signposted to 'The Sawreys'. The track climbs up a very rocky, virtually unrideable surface, for a mercifully short distance. The track quickly meets a much nicer forest road which should be followed to the **R**.

The road soon meets a wooden stile and gate arrangement and, after a very short distance, the views down Claife Heights and Wise Een Tarn come into view. Stop awhile here and muse upon the immense beauty of nature, before preparing yourself for the splendid downhill charge still to come.

4 The bridleway ahead is easy to follow as it runs gently downhill across the tops. After a short climb, the track begins to drop more steeply downhill, past another beautiful setting at Moss Eccles Tarn, then on again, until a Y-junction is met. The right branch will take you down to Near Sawrey, so if you are intending to make the Beatrix Potter experience part of your day, this would be your best option. If you are heading straight back for the ferry, you will need to take the **L** branch at the junction. This drops steeply down a rocky track then levels out to give good riding, across a ford, to pick up a tarmac drive coming down from a large house soon after the ford.

Follow the drive, downhill, to meet the main B5285 at Far Sawrey. Turn **L** up the main road, passing a hotel on the left and climbing briefly to the top of the hill at Bryers Fold. There now follows an exciting downhill run on the road, watching out for oncoming cars and the odd sharp bend, past the lakeside lane that you sped along at the start of the ride, and round the final headland back to the ferry. Excellent stuff!

Low Borrowdale & Howgill Lane

ROUTE 13 // 18.4km (11.4 miles)

If peaceful solitude in a beautiful setting is your thing, then this is for you. I have cycled this gem of a valley (not to be confused with its famous namesake near Keswick) **time after time and have yet to meet another cyclist or walker. The valley has no road along it, although the bridleway shares its lower length with a gravel track. Ahead, the Howgills rise spectacularly as the route picks up an ancient Roman road skirting the lower flanks of the Howgill Fells and on towards the market town of Sedbergh.**

This is a linear route, so arrangements will need to be made to leave a car at the end to get you home. You will find that this extra trouble is well worth the effort!

To find the starting point, follow the A6 out of Kendal, north towards Shap. After a few km, the road to Longsleddale and the The Plough Inn are passed on the left. The A6 then snakes round a few bends, passes the site of the Jungle Café (now Kendal Caravans) and climbs up the fells towards Shap. The next farm on the left is Hollowgate and just past the farm the road reaches a high point on a sharp bend to the left. Borrowdale runs off to the right here, and easy parking can be found in the large layby a few metres down the hill on the left.

Cars can be parked at the end of the route in Sedbergh (which will add about 1km to the total distance) or alternatively, there are parking spaces in the area around Lincoln's Inn Bridge on the A684 as it crosses the river Lune.

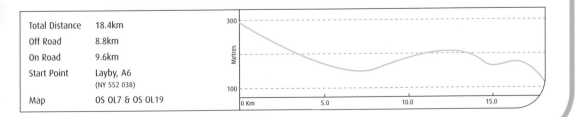

Total Distance	18.4km	
Off Road	8.8km	
On Road	9.6km	
Start Point	Layby, A6 (NY 552 038)	
Map	OS OL7 & OS OL19	

PHOTO // moving fast on Howgill Lane

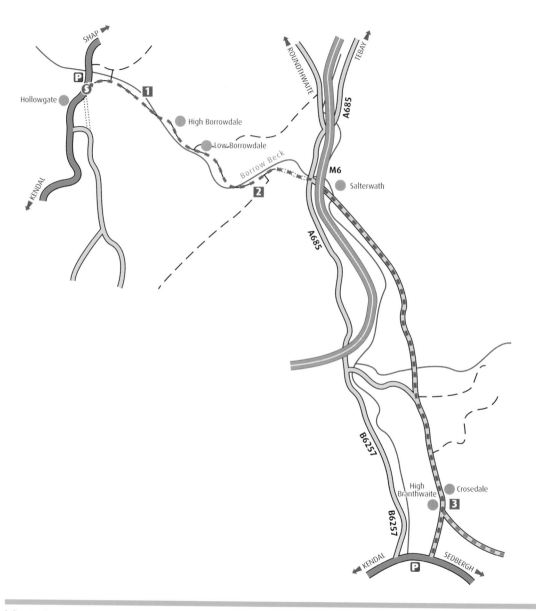

SHAP

P
⑤
Hollowgate

1

High Borrowdale

Low Borrowdale

KENDAL

Borrow Beck

2

ROUNDTHWAITE

TEBAY

A685

M6

Salterwath

A685

B6257

B6257

High
Branthwaite

Crosedale

3

KENDAL

P

SEDBERGH

The route first heads back up the hill in the direction of Kendal, to the sharp bend on the top. At this point, a rough track drops steeply down the hill to the **L** into the Borrowdale valley. Follow this track downstream, don't cross but keep to the **R** of the streamway, after 2km a small bridge is met and the bridleway crosses over to run down the **L** bank.

1 Follow the easy track, past buildings at High Borrowdale, then climb above the stream to drop back down again at Low Borrowdale farm. Turn **R**, and pass through the farmyard, following the obvious farm drive out past the buildings and off down valley again.

NB. Be careful at Low Borrowdale, because a second bridleway goes off behind the farm then climbs up the side of Roundthwaite Common. You will know if you have chosen the wrong route because you should be heading downhill, and Roundthwaite Common is most decidedly upwards!

The trail down the valley gives very enjoyable riding in beautiful situations. After a little while, a bridge is reached, and the track crosses to the **R** bank again. A short climb then follows.

2 At the top of this climb, a bridleway goes off up the fell on the **R**. This is not our way onwards, but a glance at the map will show that it gives an interesting variation as it climbs steeply up to the repeater station high on the top of Whinfell. The access road to the station can then be followed downhill and quiet lanes followed around the lower slopes of Whinfell Common and Ashstead Fell, back to the start point at the head of Borrowdale.

That is for another day however, because our (more gentle) route continues down the valley, soon meeting a tarmac surface, and eventually popping out at a T-junction with the A685 (Kendal to Tebay road).

Turn **R** (towards Kendal) then almost immediately **L** again, onto the quiet Fairmile Road. Immediately pass under the motorway and the main West Coast railway line, then follow the road down to a farm. **Don't turn right** between the farm buildings but take the road that leads off **L** to drop down to a bridge over the infant River Lune at Salterwath.

There now follows about 8km of lovely riding along Howgill Lane. The route is not without some effort however, as you find that each stream coming down off the Howgill Fells has carved out a mini ravine which needs to be descended and then climbed out of as you progress. Ignore all roads going off right and left as you pass farms at Gate House, Gate Side, Birkhaw and Crosedale. After about 8km, watch out for a farm drive on your right leading downhill to High Branthwaite, because, just past this point, the road ahead splits at a Y-junction.

3 If you have left your return transport at Sedbergh, you will need to take the **LH** fork, which climbs slightly before beginning its descent into the town. If you have parked in the area of Lincoln's Inn Bridge however, the **RH** fork is your homeward path, and this drops steeply downhill along Slack Lane and reaches the A684 at a T-junction. Turn **R** here (towards Kendal) quickly to find the parking areas mentioned at the start of this route.

clapham, norber & crummackdale

ROUTE 14 // 13.7km (8.5 miles)

Clapham is a delightful little village in North Yorkshire, nestled snugly at the base of Ingleborough and roughly mid-way between Ingleton and Settle.

The route takes advantage of low passes into unspoiled, picturesque valleys which climb steadily, on excellent tracks, to a viewpoint overlooking the looming magnificence of Ingleborough. Here on the high point will be found a stunning 360° panorama of some of the most beautiful landscape in Britain. The way back even passes Ingleborough show cave so, if you fancy a change from all that interminable sunshine, why not stop off and explore the subterranean underworld for a couple of hours?

Clapham itself has a large car park and enough shops and cafes to provide life's little essentials.

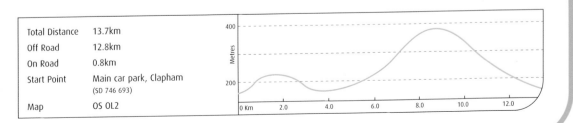

Total Distance	13.7km
Off Road	12.8km
On Road	0.8km
Start Point	Main car park, Clapham (SD 746 693)
Map	OS OL2

PHOTO // IN MY DAY BIKES ONLY HAD 3 GEARS!

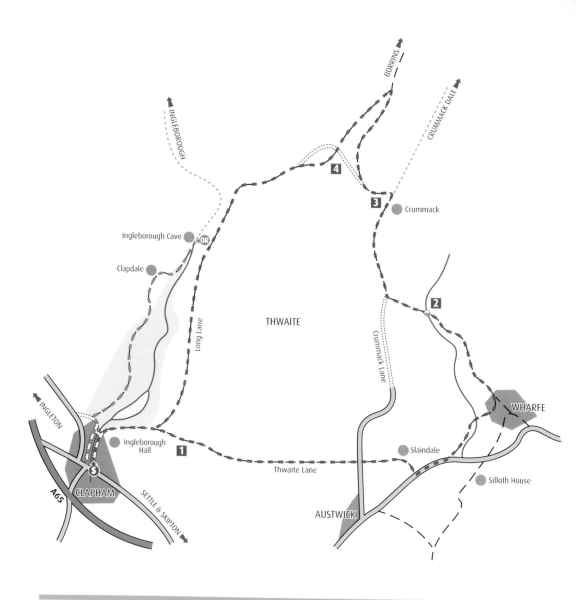

INGLEBOROUGH

BORRINS

CRUMMACK DALE

4

3 Crummack

Ingleborough Cave **OR**

Clapdale

Long Lane

THWAITE

2

WHARFE

Crummack Lane

Ingleborough Hall

1

Slaindale

Thwaite Lane

Silloth House

INGLETON

S

CLAPHAM

AUSTWICK

A65

SETTLE & SKIPTON

The ride is described from the main car park in the village and provides a very entertaining ride almost immediately from the start. Leaving the car park, turn **R** along the quiet road (past the entrance to Ingleborough Hall) and ride along towards the church. Just before the church, you need to take an unsurfaced track on the **R**. This is Thwaite Lane, part of the Pennine Bridleway. The track quickly disappears into two short tunnels. This section is understandably dark, rocky and entertaining but the surface is rideable and the tunnels short. The track now climbs steeply on a rocky surface and I must confess to not even trying to ride up it any more. A steady plod brings you out of the woods onto the more open area on the top of the hill with fine views all round.

1 The track joining from the left at this point (Long Lane) is the rocky return route but our outward journey follows the fine level track **SA**. This track gives excellent riding, either level or downhill, and usually through numerous standing pools if the weather has not been exceptionally dry. After a couple of km, you will arrive damp, muddy and blissfully happy at a point where the track crosses a very quiet tarmac road. Go **SA** over the road and follow the track as it continues down the hill opposite, to arrive even happier and muddier at another tarmac road just outside the village of Austwick. Turn **L** along the road for about 300m and take a bridleway signposted off to the **L**. This narrow bridleway climbs very gently and crosses a quaint little bridge to arrive in the hamlet of Wharfe. The road passes the first few houses until, just after a very old and quaint building, a **L** turn can be found going upwards by the side of the house. This can be a little confusing because it rather looks like the entrance to a private drive. However, immediately behind the houses the way on becomes clear, climbing steadily alongside the wall, on a track that is generally good but has one or two rocky sections that will test your riding (or your pushing) skills.

The climb isn't too long and gives way to a pleasant, downhill section leading to a ford. Now, I have seen a few people make it successfully across this ford – but I have also seen many more people get very wet in it! Bridge or ford? Man or mouse? I usually squeak meekly as I push across the bridge then guffaw loudly as the men end up in the stream!

2 Pleasant riding for a further few hundred metres meets Crummack Lane coming in from the left. Our route turns **R** at this junction to climb up the hill to Crummack Farm.

3 Keep to the **L** of the farm, passing through two signposted gates and follow the wall on the **R**, up an obvious wide track, aiming for the gate on the skyline ahead. A little before the gate, a prominent fingerpost points you up the hill to the **L**. The track is quite easy to follow, swinging round to the **L** then bearing back **R** and climbing steadily all the while. Don't be disheartened at this point! The climb can be ridden (or pushed as your legs begin to complain), and the views are superb! I usually stop frequently to look lovingly around, waxing lyrically about the scenery, while my lungs struggle to reach a state where they can go on a little further. It doesn't fool anyone of course, but the others are all so tired that they pretend to believe me just so they can have a rest as well.

The top of the hill (and the high point of the route) is met at a particularly incongruous traffic sign aimed at the 4x4 brigade. How anyone in the planning department could allow such an ugly and unnecessary construction is beyond me but it does make a useful carbuncle on the backside of humanity, which we can utilise as a waymark.

4 There is an obvious crossroads at this point on the hill. **Ignore** those tracks going right and left and instead, go **SA**, taking the downhill option. There now follows an excellent downhill run on an obvious track with some nice rocky sections ready to catch the show-offs who are going too fast. Follow the trail down, through one gate and onto a second.

The rocky track which drops down on the other side of the gate is Long Lane. This gives a long, fast, rocky and exhilarating descent until a short but steep rise brings you out into known territory again. Wrists aching, brake blocks steaming and bum smarting, you should recognise the junction as the one you passed a couple of hours ago after climbing up the first hill after the tunnels.

To return to the village, turn **R** at the junction, dropping back down through the tunnels, (careful – it's very dark in there) and turn **L** at the road to return to the car park.

Optional Route: From the gate at the top of Long Lane, a parallel track runs down the valley bottom alongside the stream issuing from Ingleborough Cave. A glance at the map shows that this track is a bridleway, starting from the mouth of Ingleborough Cave then climbing up the other side of the valley to Clapdale Farm. Once up to the farm buildings, the access track is also designated as a bridleway and this can be followed as a fast, downhill descent into Clapham village. There are a number of footpaths that can be used to get from the top of Long Lane down onto the bridleway at Ingleborough Cave. It must be stressed however, that these are FOOTPATHS and therefore your bikes can only be pushed along them until you reach the bridleway. Whether or not this optional descent is worth the trek down into the valley bottom and then the walk up the other side to the farm, is a debatable point. However, this route is so good that it would be worth doing it again sometime just to try the other descent option!

PHOTO // pete dodd and freya bloor near austwick

INGS to kentmere

ROUTE 15 // 14.4km (9 miLes)

Very popular with local mountain bikers, and for good reason, the low fells between Kentmere and Longsleddale give excellent riding on great tracks and bridleways. This circuit gives a tantalising taste of the potential of the district, taking in some of the best trails from the myriad of tracks crossing the area. Once you have got a taste for riding around the Kentmere fells, you'll be back to explore some of the many other possibilities!

This route could be started from Staveley village, or from Kentmere itself, but I find that the Watermill pub in the village of Ings (on the A591, Kendal to Windermere) is a very convenient starting point, in that there is plenty of parking (ask first if using the pub car park) and the Watermill has a very good reputation for food and refreshments.

Coming from Kendal, take the first turn off the A591 at Ings (immediately after the garage) and follow through the hamlet, past the pub, to find parking places just before the road re-joins the A591 at the other end of the village.

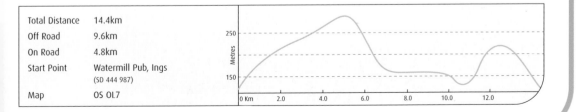

Total Distance	14.4km
Off Road	9.6km
On Road	4.8km
Start Point	Watermill Pub, Ings
	(SD 444 987)
Map	OS OL7

PHOTO // LOOSE DOUBLE-TRACK IN THE LAKES

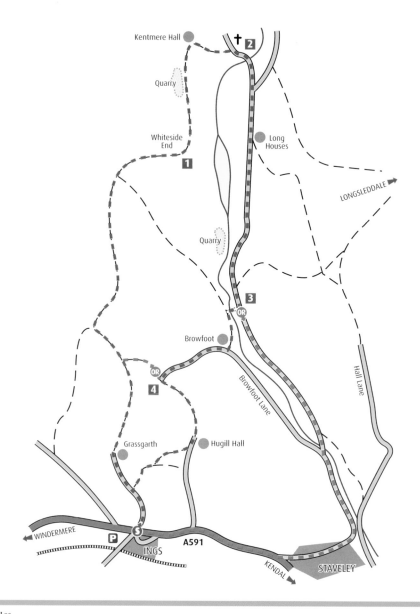

Kentmere Hall

† 2

Quarry

Whiteside
End

1

Long
Houses

LONGSLEDDALE

Quarry

3
OR

Browfoot

OR

4

Browfoot Lane

Hall Lane

Grassgarth

Hugill Hall

WINDERMERE

P

S

INGS

A591

KENDAL

STAVELEY

Our route begins by crossing the A591 at the Windermere end of Ings village and climbing steeply up the lane directly opposite, to Grassgarth and St Ann's Farm.

Follow this lane **SA** until the tarmac runs out and a bridleway takes over. After 1km of pleasant riding, another bridleway joins from the right. More of this later, but for the moment, just ignore it and carry on in the same direction as before. A few hundred metres later, another bridleway junction is reached. The left branch swings round to High House farm but we take the **RH** branch, following it over towards Kentmere. Pleasant riding now follows, although it can be very wet, muddy and slippery after rain. Eventually, a junction is reached by a sheepfold, with another bridleway going off to the **R**. Ignore this distraction (it drops down into Kentmere much further down the valley) and continue **SA** along the main track.

1 The track begins to drop steeply downwards as you meet Whiteside End and there now follows an exhilarating, rocky descent, past an old disused quarry, to arrive at the valley floor at Kentmere Hall. Follow the farm access lane to climb a small hill onto the tarmac road at Kentmere Church.

2 Turn **R** at the road for a few km of road riding back down the valley towards Staveley, passing Millriggs on the left and the entrance to the quarry works a little further along on the right. A few hundred yards further along the road from the quarry, a narrow road goes off to the **R**, across the river. At this point a decision will need to be made.

3 **Optional Route:** If your legs are gently (or otherwise) telling you that they have had quite enough for one day, then the quickest and easiest way back to the car (and your lunch) is to continue down the road into Staveley village. The road crosses the river at Scroggs Bridge, and then continues down to the old mill weir at Barley Bridge.

Don't cross the river at Barley Bridge, but continue into the village until you meet the Church and turn **R** along Brow Lane. The lane climbs gently then meets a larger road at a point where the Kendal to Windermere cycle track is signposted on the **R**. Follow the cycle track, alongside the A591 back to your car at Ings village after about 1km.

If however, you have benefitted from all those earlier bike rides and you are eager for more, then your track will head off **R** along the narrow road and over the bridge to find a bridleway going off **L** immediately afterwards. The bridleway quickly arrives at Browfoot Farm, but take care at this point, as it is very easy to go wrong by following the obvious track. The bridleway you are looking for turns off to the **R**, through the fields, immediately **before** the farm buildings. The route climbs a little then drops down again to meet a quiet tarmac road.

Turn **R** up the lane and climb steadily up (and up) the hill. Just as you are seriously regretting opting for the longer route, the lane reaches a T-junction. Both routes join up lower down the hill so either way is a possibility!

4 Turning **L** will take you down past The Heights and Hugill Hall, (ignore a bridleway coming in from the left a little further on), to join a minor road just lower down from Grassgarth and St Ann's Farm. Continue downhill (turn **L**) to meet the main road at Ings after a short descent.

Optional Route: Turning **R** at the junction quickly meets the bridleway that you slogged up at the start of this route. **Don't continue SA unless you want to do the whole circuit again!** Instead, turn back sharp **L** and reverse your outward route back down to Grassgarth and then **SA** down the tarmac road to Ings, welcome relief and a well-earned OJ.

twisteton scars
& RIBBLeHeaD viaduct

ROUTE 16 // 16.9km (10.5 miles)

Immediately north of Ingleton, between the huge whaleback of Whernside and the imposing bulk of Ingleborough, are the much less frequented, (and much lower) limestone slopes of Twisleton Scars. A bridleway runs the entire length of the scars, between Ingleton and the impressive viaduct at Ribblehead. Once the initial climb up to the top of the scars has been completed, this route gives a fantastic run, with numerous possibilities for shortening the journey if your little legs begin to flag. The return to Ingleton takes advantage of a quiet and picturesque lane along Chapel-le-Dale.

NB. The Bridleway across Scales Moor can become very boggy after rain and cycling across it in these conditions will cause inevitable damage to this vulnerable environment. The Yorkshire Dales National Park authority request that cyclists avoid riding this route if the weather has been particularly wet.

For the sake of completeness, I shall describe the ride from the square in Ingleton, but I warn you that the first section climbs the VERY steep hill of Oddies Lane. I would suggest that a much better solution would be to drive this section and take advantage of the parking possibilities at the top of the hill, around the point where the waterfall walk crosses the road between Twisleton Hall and Beezleys Farm (SD 705 749). Further parking can be found a little further along the lane at Twisleton Dale House where the farmer will allow you to park responsibly for a modest fee.

Parking on the top doesn't cut out all of the climbing however, and by the time you have plodded up Twisleton Scar End to begin the ride along the top, you may well be thanking me profusely for saving you the extra agony of the slog up the road from Ingleton!

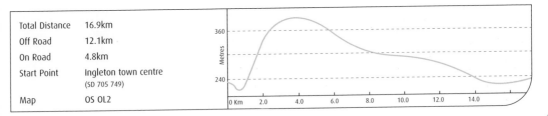

Total Distance	16.9km
Off Road	12.1km
On Road	4.8km
Start Point	Ingleton town centre (SD 705 749)
Map	OS OL2

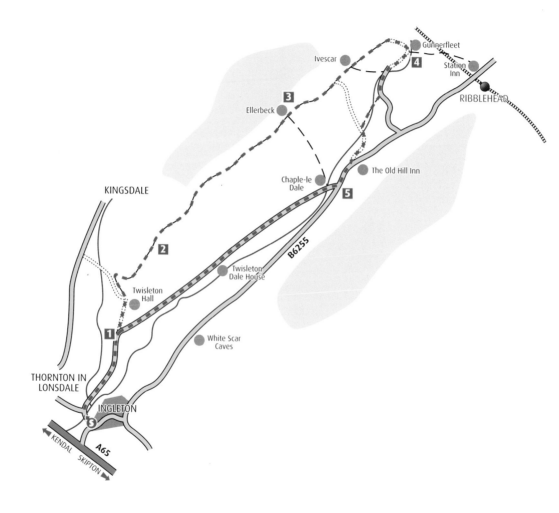

KINGSDALE

Ivescar

Gunnerfleet

4

Station Inn

RIBBLEHEAD

3

Ellerbeck

The Old Hill Inn

Chaple-le Dale

5

B6255

2

Twisleton Dale House

Twisleton Hall

White Scar Caves

1

THORNTON IN LONSDALE

INGLETON

S

KENDAL

A65

SKIPTON

From the square in Ingleton, walk against the one-way system to the church and drop down the steep hill immediately in front of it. You have now escaped from the restrictions of the one-way system and can legally-begin to ride again in the direction you wish to head. Just before the bridge over the river, a narrow lane goes off to the **R**. This is Oddies Lane. Follow this as it climbs steeply uphill, easing towards the top, until another lane goes off **L** to Twisleton Hall.

1 If you have taken my advice and wimped out of the climb up from Ingleton, you will probably be parked on the top of the hill, just past the lane up to Twisleton Hall. In this case, drop back down the road, and turn **R** through a gate to climb steadily up to the Hall on the pleasant, tarmac surface.

Follow this lane, passing through the buildings to reach a rough track at a cross roads and turn **L** along it, almost immediately passing through a gate. Once through the gate, look very carefully on the hillside on the **R** to find a vague track leaving your lane and slanting gently up the hill. This is your bridleway onto the top of Twisleton Scars. An ice-cream van can often be found parked a little further along this lane. If you reach it, (or a prominent parking area next to a gate) you have gone a little too far, (unless you were looking for a ninety-nine!) but your track can be seen zig-zagging up the fell just behind it.

The bridleway is difficult to follow in places as modern usage has created more than one route onto the tops. In reality however, there are two walls running almost directly up the fell – one to your left and another to your right. The bridleway essentially zig-zags between these two walls, picking the line of least resistance through the limestone scars onto Ewes Top. Once the steep climb is over, head generally towards the wall on your **L** to find the track again quickly, marked by a number of large cairns. Rest assured that the climbing is almost over by this point as the (now obvious) track begins to level out and then drop downwards again across Scales Moor.

2 This is fine riding in a fantastic situation. Ingleborough rises majestically on your right and the huge whaleback of Whernside looms to the left. The track is generally easy to follow as it drops more steeply downhill giving pleasant riding with the odd area of wheel-buckling limestone pavement which needs to be treated with considerable caution!

In the distance, the farm at Ellerbeck comes into view and your track heads gently downhill to pop out onto the access road just lower than the farm buildings. This is a bit of a shame however, because our next task is to climb UP the track ahead, to ride through the farm itself.

NB. If your legs have had enough at this point, it is possible to turn **R** down the farm track here, dropping down into the valley. You will soon reach the Church in Chapel-le-Dale where a **R** turn onto the minor road gives a delightfully pleasant ride, along easy terrain, back to your start point.

3 The continuation of the bridleway is very pleasant indeed and route finding is never difficult. If in doubt, remember to stick to the main track and continue roughly **SA**. A mixture of farm track and grassy fields leads through farms at Bruntscar, Broadrake, Ivescar and on towards Winterscales.

4 Just before you reach Winterscales, a farm lane turns off to the **R** down to Gunnerfleet Farm. Take this route down to the farm.

Our route homewards does not go quite as far as the Ribblehead Viaduct, but, if you wish to see it close up, look for a further bridleway on the **L**, just at the end of the farm buildings, this passes between barns and continues onwards to pass under the Viaduct and out onto the B6255 at the Station Inn. It is well worth popping along to gawp at this impressive structure before retracing your steps back to the farm at Gunnerfleet and heading for home.

5 Continuing along the farm lane from Gunnerfleet, cross a small bridge over the (normally dry) Winterscales Beck and, and continue along the lane to a cattle grid. Immediately over the cattle grid, look over at the wall on the **RH** side of the road as it rises to a corner, where a small gate can be seen. Go through this gate and follow the wall and fence on the left as it drops down the hill towards a patch of trees. An area of bare limestone is met where the dry streamway overflows in flood conditions and a series of metal gates make a barrier to prevent livestock from escaping down the streamway. To the **R** of these barriers, head through another gate into a field with a partially ruined barn on a small hill on the right. Follow the wall on the **L** to another gate which leads into a continuation of the bridleway which runs along the dry streambed. The streambed is rocky and can be slippery in places during wet weather, but it is only a short way before it pops out onto tarmac at Philpin Lane. In the unlikely event of the stream flowing along the bridleway, a dry escape route can be found by not passing through the last gate but following the fence on the **L** which runs along the field above the streamway and exits onto Philpin Lane immediately alongside the official bridleway.

Turn **L** along Philpin Lane, past a couple of farms, to reach the main road (the B6255) just after a cattle grid and a little downhill from the Old Hill Inn. Turn **R** to drop down the hill ahead but, just at the bottom, look out for a **R** turn into the minor road that runs back along Chapel-le-Dale.

Pass the church and enjoy a very pleasant ride along this beautiful valley, back to your start point in about 4km.

casterton & Barbon
via Bull pot farm
ROUTE 17 // 16km (10 miles)

Located just outside Kirkby Lonsdale, Casterton Fell is overshadowed by its larger cousins just down the road around Ingleton. While busloads of walkers follow nose-to-tail along the tourist 'motorways' leading up the Yorkshires Dales' three peaks, Casterton and Barbon Fells retain a peaceful tranquillity discovered only by a discerning few! Lower they may be, but these fells retain a grandeur all their own with the spectacular dry valley of Easegill and wonderful picnic spots alongside the beck in Barbondale. This lovely area doesn't give up its charms cheaply however; the climb up is steep and sweaty but the rewards are well worth the effort.

Start in the village of Casterton where parking is easily found. The Pheasant Inn car park seems to be a suitable meeting point if you intend to sooth your aches and pains with liquid anaesthetic at the end of the ride – but better check that the barman doesn't mind before you ride off into the sunset.

Alternatively, the ride could be started and ended at Barbon a few km up the road. It also has plenty of parking and a village pub. What more could a thirsty cyclist wish for?

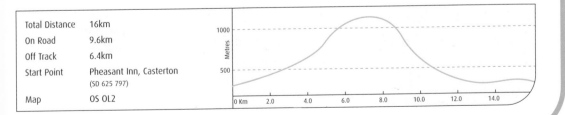

Total Distance	16km	
On Road	9.6km	
Off Track	6.4km	
Start Point	Pheasant Inn, Casterton	
	(SD 625 797)	
Map	OS OL2	

PHOTO // AUTUMN COLOURS

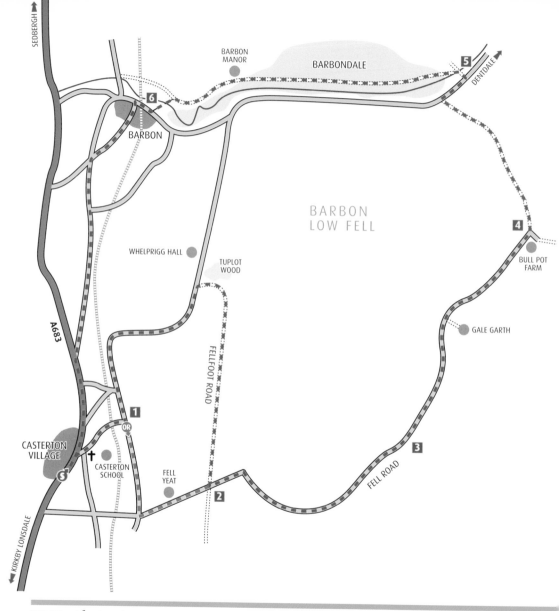

SEDBERGH

BARBON
MANOR

BARBONDALE

5

DENTDALE

6

BARBON

BARBON
LOW FELL

4

BULL POT
FARM

A683

WHELPRIGG HALL

TUPLOT
WOOD

GALE GARTH

FELLFOOT ROAD

1

OR

CASTERTON
VILLAGE

3

FELL ROAD

CASTERTON
SCHOOL

S

FELL
YEAT

2

KIRKBY LONSDALE

From the Pheasant in Casterton, go **L** out of the car park then immediately **R**, up alongside the church and through the various houses and buildings that make up Casterton School. Quickly leave the buildings behind and pass under a bridge carrying the route of a (now disused) railway.

A little aside!
This disused railway can be followed from Tebay, at the head of the Lune Valley, all the way down through Barbon and on to Ingleton. Unfortunately, there is no right of way along most of the track and many gates and fences prevent it being used by walkers or cyclists. However, if it were opened up again as a cycleway/footpath by a worthy organisation such as SUSTRANS Wow – what a route that would be! Kirkby-Stephen to Settle, mainly off-track, mainly downhill, and mostly through the upper Lune Valley. Then jump onto the Settle-Carlisle train for the uphill section back to Kirkby-Stephen. The best ride in Britain I reckon!

1 After the railway bridge, a junction is met and a decision needs to be made.
  A. (Recommended) You can add a couple of km to the route – 1km of on-road riding to come back along an excellent section of bridleway. **or**
  B. Stick to tarmac and meet the bridleway where it joins the on-road route.

Heroes taking the first option will need to turn **L** at the railway bridge junction, keep **R** at the next bridge and climb a short but steep hill past a couple of farms, arriving gasping for breath at the top. The bridleway is obvious and goes off to the **R** alongside a small wood. It is steep at first and will probably (definitely) require pushing in places - but persevere(!) – the steep bit is

quite short and the next section gives excellent riding with some rocky parts which could quite easily catch out the unwary. This bridleway simply heads back the way you have just come, to pop out onto the road where the softies who took the easier, shorter route will be waiting for you. Don't forget to stop en route to smear mud on your face before telling and re-telling tales of epic deeds and impressive crashes.

Optional Route: For the softies who wish to keep on the road, turn **R** at the junction and bear off **L** at the next junction in 700m. The road passes through a farm, which doubles as a plant nursery, then begins to climb up the hill towards Bull Pot Farm. Shortly after the farm/nursery, a bridleway is found coming in from the **L**. (It also continues onwards on the other side of the road). This is the bridleway that the fitter, keener and very smug members of the group will be limping out of shortly, only to bore you with tales of daring deeds once you get back to the pub; well, it was your choice to take the wimpish route along the road!

2 **Now comes the hard bit!** The next km is steep and unrelenting, climbing steadily up the hill towards Bull Pot Farm. On the positive side, it is on tarmac which means that you can ride the less steep bits, it is much easier to push as you're on tarmac and not mud, and the views are spectacular.

You can also impress your fellow riders with your mind-reading abilities by predicting what each member of the group will say as they join you at the top of the hill. The usual comments are always gasped out of aching lungs and tend to be rather more colourful renditions of "Crumbs, that was hard work!".

3 The views from the top of the hill are well worth the effort of climbing up there. To the right is the very impressive dry valley of Easegill. The water which created the streamway now largely disappears underground far up at the head of the valley, only to reappear mysteriously way downstream towards Cowan Bridge. Deep underneath your feet is the longest cave system in Britain – but that is for another day and a different guidebook.

Our route now undulates pleasantly along the tarmac road past a couple of isolated farmsteads and onto Bull Pot Farm at the very end of the tarmac surface. The Farm is the headquarters of the Red Rose Caving Club and your arrival will doubtless coincide with the exact moment that an ugly, hairy caver decides to drop his trousers and change into a caving suit. For this reason, it is probably better not to eat before attempting this ride.

4 From the farm, an obvious track/bridleway heads off **L** downhill towards the Barbon road. This is a truly fun descent but, from time-to-time, it is steep, rocky, boggy and testing! By the time you reach the road, your wrists will ache and your bum will be tender – but the buzz is well worth the effort. You have now had the steep and the tricky – next comes the fun!

Turn **R** along the road for a little way, over a bridge and watch out for a small footbridge over the stream on the **L** of the road. 50m before the bridge is the ford – it's your choice! Are you a (wet) man or a (dry) mouse?

5 Once over the stream, turn **L** to head off downstream and downhill, along an excellent track through the woods of Barbon Manor. This descent is fast, exciting and easy, completely obliterating any lingering memories of the slog uphill or the bum-breaking descent just endured. And just to cap it all, you're heading back to the pub!

The trail eventually climbs a small rise to break out onto tarmac. This is the course of the famous Barbon Hill climb and it would probably be a good idea to plan your ride so that it didn't coincide with a myriad of fast sports cars coming up in the opposite direction. At other times, the only danger on this descent is over-exuberance, your own incompetence or the odd suicidal sheep.

6 Follow the road down to Barbon village where it comes out just uphill from the pub. **NB:** The lower section of the tarmac track into Barbon is technically a footpath. The bridleway bears **R** by a copse of rhododendron bushes just after the first long **RH** bend. Follow the grassy farm SA across the field ahead, through a gate and into a farmyard. Pass through the farmyard onto the minor road. Turn L into Barbon village and L again to the pub. Because I am a responsible member of society, I will point out at this time the dangers of riding two wheeled machines whilst under the influence of alcoholic beverages.

You will, no doubt, be the responsible type and have shunned the possibility of drinking and riding. You will also be very thirsty and wish to retire ASAP to the starting point of the ride to quench your thirst in the local hostelry. This would be particularly important if you had left your car in the aforesaid pub car park.

If this is the case, the quickest way back to Casterton would be to turn **L** at the war memorial in Barbon village and follow this quiet road for about 1km, up a short climb, to meet the main road just outside Casterton village. Turn **L** along the main road and, upon entering the village, climb a small rise to find the pub on the **R**.

Alternatively, there are a number of bridleways and quiet country roads leading back from Barbon to Casterton which can be used as a optional return route for the super-keen!

 PHOTO // NICK COTTON, LEGENDARY CYCLING AUTHOR

keNDaL to WINDERMERE

ROUte 18 // 17.6km (10.9 mILes)

The official cycleway from Kendal to Windermere runs for most of its length directly alongside the busy A591. If your idea of a peaceful afternoon is NOT **to cycle alongside a very busy main road, breathing in enough carbon monoxide to kill an elephant, then here is an alternative. This route climbs steeply out of Kendal to cross the limestone escarpment of Scout Scar and drop down into very peaceful countryside, far away from all the noise and fumes, to reach Windermere by a series of attractive bridleways and minor roads. Lovely riding on ancient byways, giving manageable climbs and fun descents in a hugely underrated** (and largely forgotten) **locality.**

The downside to a linear route is, of course, that you will either have to leave a car at Windermere for the journey home, or catch the train back. Kendal has two railway stations. Kendal Station is at the north of the town and a short walk from the town centre. The second, Oxenholme Station, is the best place to alight for the south side of the town.

If you are leaving a car at Windermere, there are numerous car parks near the railway station – which, conveniently, is where the route ends. The station can easily be found on the left as you enter Windermere on the A591 from Kendal.

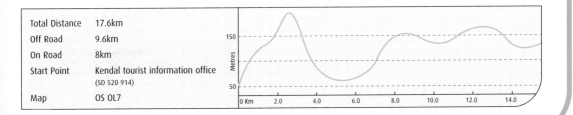

Total Distance	17.6km
Off Road	9.6km
On Road	8km
Start Point	Kendal tourist information office (SD 520 914)
Map	OS OL7

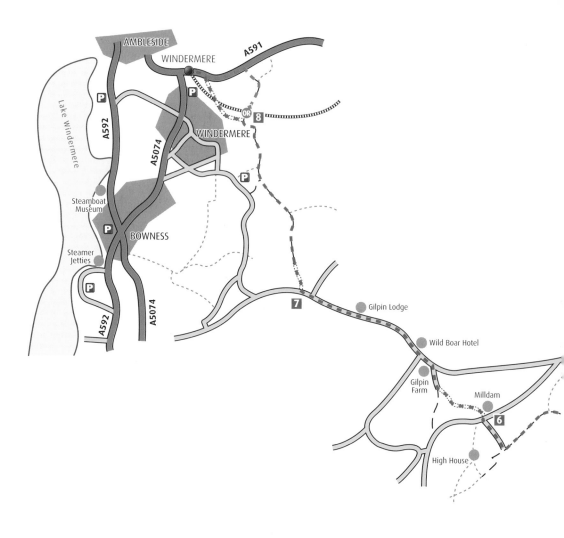

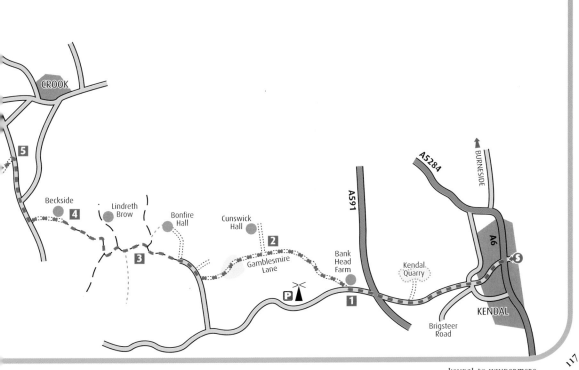

CROOK

5

Beckside
4

Lindreth
Brow

3

Bonfire
Hall

Cunswick
Hall

2

Gamblesmire
Lane

Bank
Head
Farm

1

A591

A5284

BURNESIDE

Kendal
Quarry

A6

S

KENDAL

Brigsteer
Road

The route starts from Kendal Tourist Information Office, which can be found in the Town Hall, right in the centre of town. As you walk out of the main door of the Town Hall, your route goes straight up Allhallows Lane (the road ahead of you) passing the charity shop on the left. Allhallows Lane climbs steadily, passing the Miles Thompson pub on the left, (this used to be the old bath house and has a very distinctive chimney) before turning sharp **L**. The gradient eases considerably as a grassy area is passed on the left, opposite the Rifleman's pub.

1 Continue on the same road (which now becomes Greenside) and climb steeply out of the town, past the quarry on the right and on to a bridge over the A591 Kendal bypass.

Continue, still climbing, to the first farm on the **R** (Bank Head Farm) and find a signposted bridleway on the **R** at a gate on the uphill side of the buildings. Follow this bridleway as it climbs a little to reach a gate where a footpath with a prominent signpost crosses the bridleway. Carry on through the gate onto the charmingly named Gamblesmire Lane, which gives an exciting descent over rocky terrain, through one gate and on to another.

2 The main track bears right here to drop down to Cunswick Hall. However, **SA** is a grassy track leading to an obvious wood and this is your route onwards. Drop down through the wood on a wet and rocky track, which quickly improves towards the bottom of the hill. Watch out for some cunningly concealed drainage ditches on this section!

Once out of the wood, the track climbs a little, then drops down again to another gate which meets a very quiet, tarmac road. Turn **R** along this to clatter over a cattle grid then up and over a small rise.

At the bottom of the hill, the farm lane goes right to Bonfire Hall Farm, while you need to go **SA** along a narrow bridleway, up a short hill and then up and over another similar hill to drop down to meet another farm track.

3 At the junction of farm tracks, turn **L** through the gate and follow the hedge on the **R**, down the field to cross the stream just after another gate. Follow the wall on the **R** to two gates, side by side. Take the **LH** gate and go straight up the hill to the brow. Now bear **R** and drop down the other side looking for an obvious gate in the hedge at the bottom of the field.

(The track entering through the gate on your right is the Capplerigg Lane and the Bell Hill route as it comes in from Lindreth Brow.)

With the gate from Lindreth Brow on your right, and your back to the gate you have just come through, your route onwards drops down the short hill ahead, aiming for the line of very old hedges just in front of you at the bottom. The main track heads off to the left aiming for a gate in the corner of the field but **do not** follow this route. At the line of hedges, look on your **R** for an old ruined wall and gatepost. At this point, an ancient track goes off **R** along a shallow valley. This should be followed until, a little further along, a large wooden stile becomes evident. Aim towards this stile but about 20m before reaching it, take a faint track **L** along a raised platform alongside a modern fence. This raised track quickly leads into an adjacent field where it becomes clearer as it climbs a small rise. At the top of the rise the track becomes much more obvious as it crosses the field towards a cattle grid and joins another track coming in from the right.

4 Continue **SA** and, once over the cattle grid, the track is easy to follow, leading to the farm at Beckside. Go through the farm gate and through the yard following the obvious farm drive.

Continue along the farm access road, across the stream and along a short section of tarmac to meet the quiet road from Crosthwaite to Crook. Turn **R** (towards Crook) soon to meet a Y-junction (near the parking area for a small golf club), where you take the **LH** road up the hill onto Dobby Lane. Climb steadily to the top of the hill looking out for the tarmac drive (first **L**) leading up to Crook Hall. Turn up it.

5 The track splits after a short while – keep on the **R** fork, (yes, the uphill one!) until, right on the brow of the hill and some way before reaching the farm, take an unsurfaced track leading off **L**. This track is signposted as a bridleway and as a green lane. The track drops slightly then reaches a gate. Continue on a little further to reach a T-junction, turn **L** and follow the obvious bridleway as it drops down through a number of fields (all well signposted). The track crosses a stream at the lowest point in the bottom field then goes through a gate and climbs up the next field keeping next to the wall. Follow this wall right up to the top of the field where it breaks out onto the tarmac access road to High House. Don't go up to High House but turn **R** down the road, dropping down past a couple of cottages to a T-junction at Brow Head.

6 Turn **R** here, ride just as far as the next farm (Milldam) and turn L along a signposted green lane. Pleasant riding along this brings you out to Spigot House and then **SA** down the lane takes you to the B5284 near Gilpin farm. Turn **L** onto the B5284, passing the Wild Boar Hotel and then climbing up past the Gilpin Lodge Country House Hotel, both of which will be on your right.

7 About 700m up from the Gilpin Lodge, a minor road goes off to the right. **Ignore this road** and turn **R** a few yards further on, along a tarmac road signposted for the Dales Way long distance footpath (which is also a bridleway). The track begins as tarmac but quickly becomes unsurfaced. Follow this **SA** as it drops down through fields with numerous gates, over a shallow ford, to meet another tarmac surface at a further gate. Continue to the **R**, down the hill to enter a housing estate on the outskirts of Windermere.

8 There are numerous ways from this point to reach the railway station but a simple guideline is to keep the railway line (which is only a few yards away behind the houses) generally within sight and follow it through the estate until the Booths Supermarket, the Lakeland shopping complex or the Railway Station come into view. These three complexes are right next to each other so, if you find any one of them, it is very simple to find the others!

ORTON to CROSBY RAVENSWORTH
via ODDENDALE

ROUTE 19 // 11km (6.8 miLes)

Just north of Kendal, the M6 motorway skirts the Howgill Fells as it passes through the Lune Gorge. This must be one of the most scenic stretches of motorway in the country as the M6 starts its long, laborious climb from Tebay up to Shap summit. Our route traverses the moorland fells to the east of the motorway and, although you can actually see the M6 from one or two viewpoints on the route, the rugged conditions and isolated situations give this ride a real wilderness quality. Peaty moorland trails, rocky tracks, fast singletrack descents and barely a gate in sight – this route will definitely leave you yearning for more.

To find the starting point, leave the M6 at Junction 38 (Tebay) and take the B6260 through Old Tebay to Orton village. Just past the pub in Orton, leave the main road and take the B6261 (signed 'M6' and 'Shap') which bears off left. Climb gently out of the village for about 750m to where the B6261 turns sharp right and two minor roads go off to the left. This is the starting point for the route and plenty of parking can be found around the junction.

Total Distance	17.6km	
Off Road	14.4km	
On Road	3.2km	
Start Point	Road junction NR. Orton (NY 615 081)	
Map	OS OL19 & OL5	

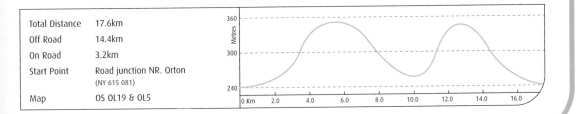

PHOTO // tom fenton, pete dodd, rosemary lakin – a 'family' of mtb bikers

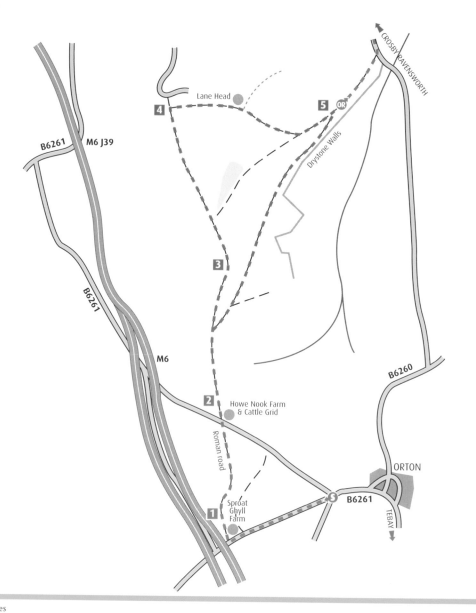

CROSBY RAVENSWORTH

B6261   M6 J39

B6261

M6

B6260

Lane Head

4

5 OR

Drystone Walls

3

2 Howe Nook Farm
      & Cattle Grid

Roman road

ORTON

S B6261

1 Sproat
      Ghyll
      Farm

TEBAY

Our route takes the minor road which heads uphill (but you just knew that it would, didn't you!). With your back to the road you have just driven up from Orton, take the minor road on your **R** (actually more or less **SA**).

The climb is short and soon gives way to a downhill section past farms at Moor House and Sproat Ghyll. Just before the farm buildings at Sproat Ghyll, a signposted bridleway crosses the road. Ignore these distractions and carry on **SA**, past the farm, watching out carefully for another bridleway on the **R**, just past the farm buildings but before the motorway flyover is reached. This bridleway does not have a sign at the moment but it is easy to spot. From the road, climb a slight rise up to a metal gate and the bridleway can be seen continuing onwards, past the farm buildings.

1 Follow the bridleway as it climbs gently, with a wall on your right. The boggy farm area is soon left behind as a little height is gained. After a short distance, the wall turns 90° sharp right while the track breaks away from it, bearing off to the **R** across open moorland on a good, easy to follow, trail. Easy riding for a short distance brings you to another wall with a farm gate.

There is an understandable tendency here to look at the well-graded farm track in the next field and to assume that this is the Roman road which you have been heading towards. Unfortunately, life is not always that simple! You are indeed heading for a Roman road, which you will follow for a considerable way; but it is on this side of the wall you have just met, and is, in fact, that miserable little track running alongside the wall and off into the distance. So much for the Roman feats of ingenuity and engineering skill. Having said that, I suppose it has been out of use for a little while!

Although uphill, the track is easy to ride and clear to follow as it runs alongside the wall for 1km to meet the B6261 coming up from Orton. Once on the road, turn **L** (away from the cattle grid) then almost immediately **R** onto the farm access drive to Howe Nook. At the farm buildings ahead, the bridleway leaves the farm track to head straight up the hill in front of you on a very obvious gravel track.

2 The track climbs steadily around the flank of the hill. The riding is mainly good with one or two sections of boggy or rutted trail. Once on the top of the climb, the main trail heads off to the **R** and another obvious track goes straight on, up another short climb ahead. The **RH** track is your return path to this junction, so I'm sorry to have to say that your route onwards is up the hill ahead. This section of track is rutted and boggy in places, but persevere, very enjoyable riding is just over the crest of the rise ahead!

3 Good riding brings you to the top of the hill and a fine viewpoint looking down the other side. You can see a large, walled enclosure ahead to the left of the track and, a little nearer, a long copse of trees to the right. Our route heads downhill, between these two features, aiming to pass alongside the **RH** boundary wall of the walled enclosure, called Potrigg.

4 From Potrigg, the track has an excellent riding surface as it runs gently downhill, with a plantation on the left, towards Oddendale. As the farm buildings in Oddendale are approached, watch carefully for a bridleway on the **R**. This bridleway turns back sharply in the direction you have just come from, but then quickly turns **L** to follow the line of trees and drystone walling above the houses and buildings.

5 Good riding along a clear track follows this wall for about 1km until the main track turns sharp left, through a gate, and down to an old farm cottage (Lane Head). Don't follow the lane down, but instead bear **R** across the fell, aiming for the walled enclosure on top of the rise ahead. The track follows parallel to the walls on the **L**, giving an excellent downhill run towards Crosby Ravensworth.

If your intention is to visit Crosby Ravensworth, this track should be followed downhill, along the curiously named 'Slack Randy' and out onto the road at Town Head. A **L** turn here continues down into the village where all the usual facilities can be enjoyed. Once your various desires have been sated, return along the same route to climb back up Slack Randy and find the route homewards.

If you are not planning to visit Crosby Ravensworth, pay careful attention as you are zooming down Slack Randy with the wall to your **L**. You will, no doubt, notice that the walls across the field to your right are steadily coming closer as they funnel you down the fell-side. Your aim is to cross over to the **RH** wall at the first opportunity because your route home follows that wall uphill, and every metre you drop down Slack Randy, is another metre you have to climb back up again as you return. The two converging tracks eventually meet, allowing you to turn back sharply in the direction you have just come and start the uphill trudge to the top of the hill again.

The track is easy to ride and follows closely to the wall, which is now on your left. Eventually, the wall turns sharp left, leaving open fell ahead and a confusing assortment of vague tracks and trails leading off in numerous directions. The secret here is to pretend that the wall you have just been following continues across the fell side and then you continue to ride in the same direction. This should take you somewhere just to the **L** of a solitary tree on the small hill ahead and then keep onwards, always in the same general direction, along the best trail you can find!

This area can be a little confusing because of the numerous tracks, but remember that you are heading back parallel to the track that you came along on the outward journey and, at this point, that outward trail is only 100 or 200m across the fell to the right. If you look in the distance to your right at this point, you will see a hill with a distinctive rock outcrop on its summit. Generally heading diagonally towards this hill will mean that you must come across familiar territory very soon. Other landmarks to watch out for are the walled enclosure of Potrigg and the long copse of trees that you passed a little while ago.

Meeting the outward route once again, turn **L** along it to drop back down to the road and cattle grid at Howe Nook. Depending on how your bum is feeling at this point, the Roman road can be followed back the way you came earlier in the day or, alternatively, turn **L** down the road, cross the cattle grid and follow the B6261 back down to your car in 1km or 2.

CROSBY RAVENSWORTH to APPLEBY

ROUTE 20 // 23.2km (14.6 mILes)

This part of Cumbria is just a little further away from the main tourist areas and consequently receives fewer visits. The result is a perfect area for walking and cycling; lots of bridleways, lots of peaceful lanes and not many people using them. This route begins in the attractive village of Crosby Ravensworth, looping round to the market town of Appleby via the ford at the beautiful Rutter Falls and then returning via Maulds Meaburn. It is the last route in this guide because it includes a couple of steep climbs and it is a little longer than the earlier routes. Don't be discouraged by this however, there are steeper climbs in the book, and your new-found fitness should see you cope with the distance without any real problems!

To reach Orton village, leave the M6 at junction 38 (Tebay) and take the B6260 (left at the roundabout) through Old Tebay.

Once in Orton, follow the B6260 towards Appleby and Crosby Ravensworth, heading north out of the village as it climbs up Orton Scar to a cattle grid on the summit. Just after the cattle grid, the road to Crosby Ravensworth goes off to the **L**, dropping 5km down the valley into the village. The village is somewhat linear in nature, so your run into town will take you past the pub and on towards the church. There are plenty of places for parking in the village.

Total Distance	23.2km	
Off Road	8.8km	
On Road	14.4km	
Start Point	Crossby Ravensworth (NY 621 147)	
Map	OS OL19	

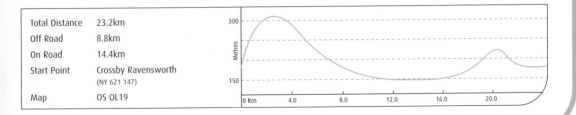

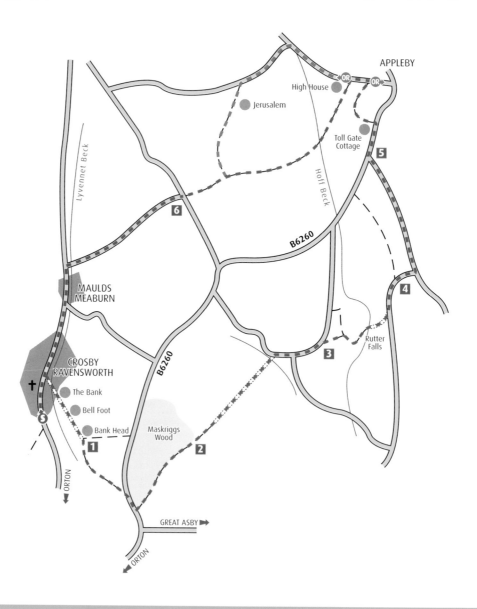

APPLEBY

High House

Jerusalem

Toll Gate
Cottage

OR **OR**

5

Hoff Beck

Lyvennet Beck

6

B6260

4

Rutter
Falls

MAULDS
MEABURN

3

CROSBY
RAVENSWORTH

B6260

5

The Bank

Bell Foot

Bank Head

Maskriggs
Wood

1

2

ORTON

GREAT ASBY ➤

ORTON

Your ride begins by heading down towards the church. Alongside the churchyard, the road crosses the beck in a very attractive setting. Only a few metres further on, take the minor road on the **R**, across another bridge over Lyvennet Beck and past Low Row on the left.

You should now be on a very quiet lane which begins to climb. As you might now be expecting, the climb is steep and prolonged. Climb (or push if you like) steadily past farms at The Bank and Bell Foot until you reach a cattle grid, and the road breaks out into more open countryside. Climb more gently now, with fine views, up to the end of the road at the farm at Bank Head.

1 The road ends abruptly in a grassy area alongside the farm, with a number of tracks heading off in various directions. The byway you need to follow is the track heading diagonally **L**, uphill, aiming for the wall corner up on the skyline, just beyond the solitary tree. Once you decide which track is your track, the way ahead is easy to follow as it climbs again, and then levels out as it reaches the top of the hill. Follow the pleasant track around to the **L**, keeping to the **L** of the small copse of trees ahead, then continue easily along a grassy trail, up to the main B6260 (Orton to Appleby) road.

Turn **R** onto the B6260 (towards Orton) immediately dropping down a small hill. Watch out carefully here because your bridleway onwards is just at the base of the hill on the left and is currently unmarked, although very easy to spot. If you reach a sharp right-hand bend on the B6260, with a minor road going off to Great Asby you have gone too far and missed your bridleway!

The bridleway gives easy riding downhill to a gate. Once through the gate, the track disappears in the next field, but by keeping roughly parallel with the wall on your left, a short climb alongside the wood will bring you to another gate. In the next field, head diagonally **R** towards the **RH** corner where a signposted gate allows access to Maskriggs Wood. The track is now easy to follow but can be muddy and boggy depending on recent weather conditions and the amount of forestry traffic it has been carrying.

2 Keep riding **SA** and the wood gives way to open countryside in a farm area with barns. The route ahead continues through a further gate, to a junction of a number of tracks. Ignore the track going off downhill and head towards the higher route, which runs along the top of a small copse, between two walls. Just before the wood, an obvious track goes through a gate on your left but ignore this also. Our lane runs between the two walls for a short distance then breaks out into open fields, on a good track aiming for Hardings Wood just ahead. More easy riding follows with fantastic views of the Pennines ahead, until the track meets a broken concrete road surface at a locked gate with a smaller, unlocked gate to one side.

There now follows a great downhill run as the broken concrete road surface quickly improves to tarmac and, just beyond an attractive bridge, a road junction is met at the hamlet of Drybeck. Turn **R** at the junction and keep **L** at the next junction (where a lane goes off right). Climb gently past Drybeck Hall (on your left) until an obvious lane on the **R** is found at Haybanks.

3 This lane is a public byway and gives excellent riding until a junction is reached. Take the **RH** branch at the junction and continue **SA** on the track to enjoy more good riding, with excellent views, until a steep descent drops down to a very attractive situation at Rutter Falls. An easily rideable ford crosses Hoff Beck at this point but there is also a bridge for the softies! Rutter Mill is a very photogenic spot and you will no doubt want to stop here for refreshments at the small teashop which opens during the summer months.

Photographs taken and appetites sated, cross the beck and head off up the short climb on the other side. After a short distance, Broadmire Road is met and a **L** turn here takes you along this busier road towards your final destination.

4 At a bend in the road ahead, the more observant of you may notice a bridleway going off to the **L**, and a glance at the map will confirm that it is heading in the direction you wish to go. I cannot recommend this route however: it is boggy, indistinct and just damned hard work as it crosses ploughed farmland with no real riding surface. If however, you are a purist and want to give it a go, then please carry on – the route finding is relatively easy as it crosses fields to Lookingflatt Farm, then goes through the farmyard before crossing more open fields to emerge on the B6260 near Friendship farm.

The more easy-going of us will ignore this esoteric gem and choose instead to continue along Broadmire Road to a T-junction. A **L** turn here gives an undulating ride, through pleasant countryside for about 1km to meet the B6260 at Burrells.

5 Turn **R** onto the B6260 towards Appleby but look out on the **L** after about 800m for the whitewashed Toll Gate Cottage. Immediately beyond the cottage, a signposted bridleway goes off **L** and gives an alternative approach to the town. The track gives easy riding to a junction with a number of farm gates. Turn **R** through a small gate with a bridleway marker and go down a narrow lane between hedges, soon joining up with a farm lane and leading out onto tarmac again on the outskirts of the town.

Optional Route: Those of you wishing to visit Appleby should turn **R** here and quickly meet the B6260 which can be followed to the **L**, rising up alongside the castle walls into the town centre. Remember your route back to the last bridleway junction however, because the route back to Crosby Ravensworth will be described from that point.

The homeward route turns **L** onto a quiet road, leading steadily uphill to a clearly marked bridleway on the **L**, after about 300m, just before High House Farm. This bridleway can be very muddy and difficult to ride as it crosses fields to Bandley Bridge and then climbs through farmland to a junction with another bridleway coming in from Jerusalem Farm, after about 3km.

Optional Route: If you look at the High House Farm bridleway and decide that it is not to your taste, there is an optional route available. Continue along the road past the farm and downhill into Colby village. Cross the bridge and climb up the hill beyond, then take the minor road on the **L**. This road climbs steeply up to a bridleway and lane on the **L** leading to a farm called Jerusalem . (They must grow artichokes.) Follow this lane through the farm and pick up the bridleway leading on beyond. The bridleway is easy to follow if you look carefully for the waymarks and it eventually meets up with the other bridleway from High House Farm.

Whichever way you opted to take, from the junction of bridleways, the main track is obvious as it heads down a small hill and up the other side on a good farm track. (**SA** if you have come from High House Farm; turn **R** if you have come from Jerusalem Farm.) After about 1km, you will reach the road to Long Rigg.

6 Going **SA** over at this junction (signposted Maulds Meaburn) gives pleasant riding on a very quiet lane. After a weary slog up a long hill comes a fine downhill descent to cross Lyvennett Beck on the outskirts of Maulds Meaburn. A **L** turn here takes you through this attractive village and up a short climb at the other end (ignoring the roads going off to the left in the village).

Continue along this pleasant road for another km or so to enter Crosby Ravensworth at the end of your longer-than-usual ride, and a well earned rest.

"britain's **best selling** mountain biking guides"

Vertebrate Graphics – your route to the best trails in the UK

Vertebrate Graphics' guidebooks are a best-selling series of user-friendly guides to the finest mountain biking in the country.

They take you to the sweetest moorland singletrack, the most exciting downhills and the scariest climbs and on routes ranging from short excursions for novices right through to 80km long techno-fests for experts. With 'top ten' descents, climbs and singletracks, clear mapping and colour photography throughout, these best-selling titles contain something for every rider, no matter who they are.

"one of the best guides... we have come across"
singletrackworld.com

"The maps and photos are top notch. Vertebrate have been in the game long enough to be market leaders."
Planetfear.com

appendices

tourist information offices

Ambleside   01539 432 582
amblesidetic@southlakeland.gov.uk

Appleby   01768 351 177
tic@applebytowncouncil.fsnet.co.uk

Bowness   01539 442 895
bownesstic@lakeland.gov.uk

Ingleton   01524 241 049
ingletontic@hotmail.com

Kendal   01539 725 758
kendaltic@southlakeland.gov.uk

Kirkby Lonsdale   01524 271 437
kltic@southlakeland.gov.uk

Sedbergh   01539 620 125
tic@sedbergh.org.uk

Settle   01729 825 192
settle@ytbtic.co.uk

Windermere   01539 446 499
windermeretic@southlakeland.gov.uk

bike shops

Ambleside   Biketreks, Compston Road
01539 431 505

Ghyllside cycles, The Slack
01539 433 592

Ingleton   Inglesports, Main Street
(Limited selection of spares)
01524 241 146

Kendal   Askew Cycles, Wildman Street
01539 728 057

Bruce's Bikes, 9 Kirkland
01539 727 230

Settle   The Station Yard
01729 822 216
www.settlecycles.co.uk

Staveley   Millennium Cycles, Crook Road
01539 821 167

Wheelbase, Staveley Mill yard
0870 600 3435 or 01539 821 443

bike hire

Ambleside	Biketreks, Compston Road 01539 431 505
	Ghyllside Cycles, The Slack 01539 433 592
Grizedale	Grizedale Mountain Bikes 01229 860 369
Ingleton	Howsons, Main Street 01524 241 422
Staveley	Millennium Cycles, Crook Road 01539 821 167
	Wheelbase, Mill Yard 0870 600 3435 or 01539 821 443

weather

BBC	www.bbc.co.uk/weather
Metro Office	www.metoffice.com

outdoor equipment/clothing

Ambleside	The Climbers Shop, Compston Corner 01539 432 297
	Gaynor Sports, Market Cross 01539 433 305
	Rock and Run, 3-4 Cheapside 01539 433 660
Clapham	Homebarn, Church Avenue 01524 251 162
Grasmere	Mountain High, College Street 015394 35417
Ingleton	Bernies, 4 Main Street 01524 241 802
	Inglesport, Main Street 01524 241 146
Kendal	Kendal Camping Centre 01539 561 177
	Kendal Sports, 28-30 Stramongate 01539 721 554
	Kentdale Outdoors, Market Place 01539 729 188
	Pete Bland Sports, 34a Kirkland 01539 731 012
Sedbergh	Sedbergh Outdoor Leisure, 83 Main St. 01539 621 898
Staveley	Lakeland Great Outdoors, Plantation Br. 01539 821 697

PUBS

Ambleside, **Settle**, **Windermere** Pubs everywhere!

Appleby
The Grapes
01768 351 407

The Royal Oak
01768 351 463

The White Hart Hotel
01768 351 598

Austwick
The Game Cock Inn
01524 251 226

Barbon
The Barbon Inn
01524 276 223

Bowland Bridge
The Hare & Hounds
01539 568 333

The Masons Arms
01539 568 486

Brigsteer
The Wheatsheaf
01539 568 254

Casterton
The Pheasant Inn
01524 271 230

Chapel-le-Dale
The Old Hill Inn
01524 241 256

Clapham
The New Inn
01524 251 203

Crook
The Sun Inn
01539 821 351

Crosby Ravensworth
The Butcher's Arms
01931 715 202

Ingleton
The Marton Arms
01524 241 281

Ings
The Watermill
01539 821 309

Kendal
The Punch Bowl
01539 560 267

The Station Inn
01539 724 094

Kirkby Lonsdale
The Orange Tree
01524 271 716

The Snooty Fox
01524 271 308

The Sun Hotel
01524 271 965

Orton
The George Hotel
01539 624 229

Far Sawrey
The Sawrey Hotel
01539 446 442

Near Sawrey
Tower Bank Arms
01539 436 334

Sedbergh
The Dalesman
01539 621 183

Sizergh
The Strickland Arms
01539 561 010

Staveley
The Eagle & Child
01539 821 320

Troutbeck
The Queens Head Hotel
01539 432 174

cafes

We can't possibly list all the cafes in the area, so here are just a few:

Ambleside, **Kendal**, **Settle**, **Windermere** – there really are too many to list in these towns, and they aren't hard to spot! Go and have a look for yourselves!

Ingleton	Bernies, 4 Main Street 015242 41802
	Inglesport, Main Street 015242 41146
Staveley	Wilf's Café 01539 822329

accommodation

Youth Hostels	www.yha.org.uk for more
Kendal	0870 770 5892
Ambleside	0870 770 5672
Windermere	0870 770 6094
Ingleton	0870 770 5880
Dentdale	0870 770 5790
Stainforth	0870 770 6046

hotels, self-catering and b&b

The Dales and the Lakes are dotted with hotels, B&B's, bunkhouses and cottages to hire. There is somewhere to stay in every town. Your best bet have a look on the websites listed later in this section, or to contact the Tourist Information Centre nearest to where you plan to ride.

camping

There are campsites dotted all over the area, ranging from the basic (a field with a toilet) to full-on swimming-pool equipped caravan sites. Again, try the Tourist Information Centres or pick one of the maps we've suggested and look for the campsite symbols.

other publications/websites

www.v-graphics.co.uk/publications

www.lakelandgateway.info

www.lake-district.com

www.yorkshiredales.org.uk

www.yorkshire-dales.com

www.mtbthedales.org.uk

Traffic-Free Cycle Trails, Nick Cotton

Where to Mountain Bike in Britain, Nicky Crowther

Yorkshire Dales Mountain Biking – South Dales, Nick Cotton

Yorkshire Dales Mountain Biking – North Dales, Nick Cotton

about the author

Keith Bradbury has lived and worked in Kendal for 24 years. His appalling level of fitness has ensured that he has an unmatched knowledge of the lowest hills, shortest climbs, longest downhill runs, and convenient short cuts in the area.

In his years of pottering through the beautifully quiet, unknown parts of south Lakeland and the northern Dales, he has squelched through bogs, fought with farm dogs and clambered through nettle-strewn quagmires that looked so inviting on the map. He vowed never to ride those trails again and promptly rejected them for ever, ensuring that no-one else need suffer similar levels of pain, anger and despair. And the reason for this selfless devotion to duty? It gets him out of doing the ironing!

The result is a book of pleasant, manageable cycle rides which will not over-exert even the most unfit cyclist. Believe me, if Keith can do it, you can too! Have fun.

acknowledgements

Thanks Mike, Chris, Will, Dean and Geoff; the hardy band of 'grumpy old men' who accompanied me through winter, summer, sunshine and rain. We have put the world to rights many times over the years... but still nobody listens!

Also, thanks to Vertebrate Graphics team for guiding me through the publishing process and producing such a stunning design.

Andy Heading, for his excellent photography, and Heather Bradbury, Mike Russell, Nick Cotton, Pete Dodd, Clair Lloyd, Jon Barton, Ben Eagle, Freya Bloor and Rosemary Lakin for providing Andy with something to photograph.

dedication

To Alison, Will and Heather. For being there when it matters!

about the photographer

Despite regular trips oop north over the years (mainly for Polaris and Trailquest events), Andy's lasting memory of the Yorkshire Dales was getting two 'volunteers' to dress up as Wallace and Gromit for a cheesy Wensleydale photo-feature. Since photographing this guide, he's realised there's much more to Yorkshire than cursing and were-rabbits, and looks forward to biking there again soon. In the meantime, he's official photographer to the European Athletic Association, and lives in a cheese-free zone in Matlock, Derbyshire.

vertebrate graphics

At Vertebrate Graphics, communication design is at the heart of all we do, from the creation of logos and identities to the development and hosting of powerful websites and email-based marketing. On the way, we can fulfil all of our clients' graphic design needs, large or small, including brochures, packaging, stationery ranges and advertising. In addition, for companies that need a 360° approach to their marketing communications, we offer design and production for point-of-purchase and the retail environment.

Vertebrate Publishing specialises in the design and production of prestigious illustrated outdoor books and guides, and we are the name behind many of the leading outdoor leisure titles in Britain. These include Hill Walking, the best-selling outdoor instruction book, and the mountain bike guide Dark Peak Mountain Biking, as well as some of Britain's best known climbing and walking guidebooks. We publish our own titles and also welcome enquiries from individual authors.

If you would like to know more, why not visit our website: **www.v-graphics.co.uk** or email **info@v-graphics.co.uk**